Russia's War Against Ukraine

Russia's War Against Ukraine

GWENDOLYN SASSE

polity

Originally published in German as *Der Krieg gegen die Ukraine. Hintergründe, Ereignisse, Folgen*
Copyright © Verlag C.H.Beck oHG, München 2022.

This translation © Polity Press, 2023

Excerpts from *Sky Above Kharkiv* © 2022 by Serhiy Zhadan and
Suhrkamp Verlag Berlin. English translation © 2023 by Reilly Costigan-Humes
and Isaac Stackhouse Wheeler

Polity Press
65 Bridge Street
Cambridge CB2 1UR, UK

Polity Press
111 River Street
Hoboken, NJ 07030, USA

ISBN-13: 978-1-5095-6059-2
ISBN-13: 978-1-5095-6060-8(pb)

A catalogue record for this book is available from the British Library.

Library of Congress Control Number: 2023934602

Typeset in 11 on 14pt Warnock Pro
by Cheshire Typesetting Ltd, Cuddington, Cheshire
Printed and bound in Great Britain by TJ Books Ltd, Padstow, Cornwall

The publisher has used its best endeavours to ensure that the URLs for external
websites referred to in this book are correct and active at the time of going to
press. However, the publisher has no responsibility for the websites and can
make no guarantee that a site will remain live or that the content is or will remain
appropriate.

Every effort has been made to trace all copyright holders, but if any have been
overlooked the publisher will be pleased to include any necessary credits in any
subsequent reprint or edition.

For further information on Polity, visit our website:
politybooks.com

For my friends and colleagues in and from Ukraine
For my daughter Nora, and for Jim

Contents

Preface

This book has been written in the midst of war. An earlier German edition was published in October 2022 by C.H.Beck. This new edition in English analyses developments up to April 2023. As I am translating and updating the text, the war is once again concentrated in the Donbas region of eastern Ukraine. Around the city of Bakhmut, Russian and Ukrainian forces are fighting a brutal war of attrition with big losses on both sides. Overall, estimates put the current death toll at over 100,000 for both the Russians and the Ukrainians. The Ukrainian forces currently risk becoming trapped in Bakhmut, but the Ukrainian military command has not given up on the city. Their hope is to tie down Russian forces for as long as possible ahead of launching new offensives with Western military support – in particular new main battle tanks supplied by a number of NATO countries. At regular intervals, the Russian army continues its missile strikes against cities and infrastructure across the whole of Ukraine. On 17 March 2023, the International Criminal Court in the Hague issued an arrest warrant for Russian President Vladimir Putin and Maria Lvova-Belova, Russia's Commissioner for Children's Rights, in connection with the deportation of children from Ukraine to Russia.

The EU and NATO have demonstrated an unprecedented degree of unity with regards to both sanctions against Russia and military and financial assistance for Ukraine. There have been debates about the type, sequencing and effectiveness of the sanctions against Russia, as well as the scope and pace of Western arms supplies to Ukraine. The Central and East European member states of the EU and NATO have set the tone of the debate, while the United States has played the crucial role in forging a Western response. The scenario of a protracted war – in which Ukraine has no basis for negotiations and Russia no interest in them – has been emerging. Whether the EU and NATO consensus on continued support for Ukraine can be maintained over the course of a long war of attrition cannot be taken for granted in the context of growing domestic discontent over fiscal pressures and policy priorities. Moreover, the global repercussions of the war are becoming ever more apparent.

From the start, the Russian state rhetoric, the scale of destruction, the war crimes committed by the invading troops and the occupation of further Ukrainian territories have left no doubt about what Russia under President Putin is after: the destruction of the Ukrainian state and the Ukrainian nation. Thus, it is also a war against ideas such as sovereignty, territorial integrity, democracy and peaceful coexistence in Europe.

This compact book is an attempt to take stock in face of the daily breathlessness of the war. It does not describe all the developments since February 2022 in detail, but rather provides the context and thinks about the war against a broader backdrop. While it draws on social science research on Ukraine and Russia, it is written for a non-academic audience. Research on Ukraine has been neither visible enough in the social sciences nor in the wider public discourse, but it is essential for understanding the current developments. Though there is uncertainty about the end of the war and its aftermath, certainty about it in the form of documentation and contextualization is an indispensable prerequisite. Hopefully, this book will contribute to a better understanding of Russia's war against Ukraine.

How can this war be explained? Why and against what is Russia waging it, and why now? What explains the strength of Ukraine's military and civil resistance, which has surprised not only Putin and the Russian armed forces but also many Western observers? These are big questions for such a short book. It deliberately does not start with Putin's order to attack the whole of Ukraine on 24 February 2022 or with a chronology of events since then. Instead, it begins with Ukraine's independence and the challenges the Ukrainian state has had to face since 1991 in terms of its territorial integrity, its transformation and its domestic and foreign policy orientation. The multifaceted concept of identity runs like a thread throughout this book: from Ukrainian national and state independence to the role of ethnic, linguistic and regional identities, to the overarching civic identity tied to the Ukrainian state and its political decision for democracy and integration into Western institutions. These are the developments that the authoritarian system under Vladimir Putin reacted to with war – from the annexation of Crimea and the war in Donbas to the large-scale invasion since February 2022.

The book deliberately focuses on social and political dynamics that have been documented in the scholarship but were largely unknown beyond academia and are often still misunderstood even in the current war context. The drive in Ukrainian society for pro-democratic political change plays a critical role. It manifested itself in repeated cycles of mass protests and became the basis for the current military and civil resistance. The fact that Ukraine did not figure on the mental horizon of most people in the West until 2022 has a lot to do with an undifferentiated view that, more than thirty years after the break-up of the Soviet Union in 1991, equated the USSR with Russia. This view tended to ignore the transformations of the other states emerging from the Soviet Union. The imperialism of the Russian Empire and the Soviet Union continues to influence Western perspectives on the region and the terminology used to classify it. For this reason, I deliberately avoid using the adjective 'post-Soviet', which reduces Ukraine and an entire region to the experiences and legacies of the Soviet Union.

The list of those who have sharpened my view of Ukraine is too long to reproduce here in full. I would like to thank at least those colleagues with whom I have cooperated most closely for many years in my research on Ukraine: Olga Onuch, Henry Hale, Volodymyr Kulyk and the team at the Kyiv International Institute of Sociology (KIIS). Along my academic path, I owe important insights reflected in this book to Roman Szporluk, Margot Light, Dominic Lieven, James Hughes, Chris Binns, Mark Beissinger, Serhii Plokhy, Graeme Robertson and Sam Greene. Two large collaborative projects – the Open Research Area-funded project MOBILISE (German Research Foundation, DFG-Project-ID: 396856214) and the Cluster of Excellence project 'Contestations of the Liberal Script', funded by the German Research Foundation (EXC 2055, Project-ID 390715649) – have placed my research on Ukraine in a productive comparative framework in recent years. I am also grateful for the research assistance provided by Alice Lackner in several of my Ukraine-related projects at ZOiS, and for Nikol Levova's help in compiling the bibliography. I would like to thank my publisher C.H.Beck, especially Sebastian Ullrich, for commissioning the original German edition; Polity Press, especially John Thompson, for pursuing this English-language edition, and Tim Clark for his copy-editing. I am grateful to James Hughes for casting his critical eye over my translation and adaptation of the book. Most importantly, Jim and Nora deserve heartfelt thanks for the support and strength they have given me since 24 February 2022 in these unbelievably intense and sad times.

Maps

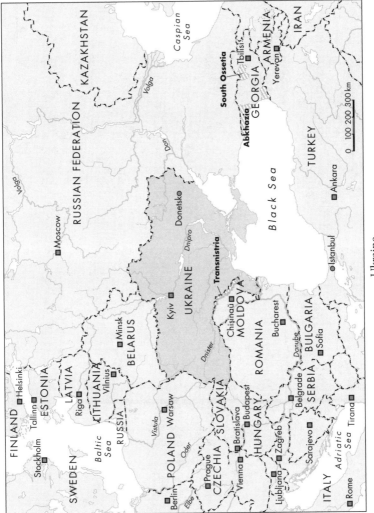

Ukraine

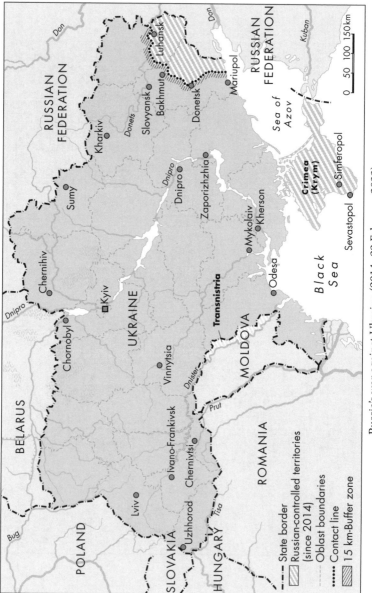

Russia's war against Ukraine (2014–23 February 2022)

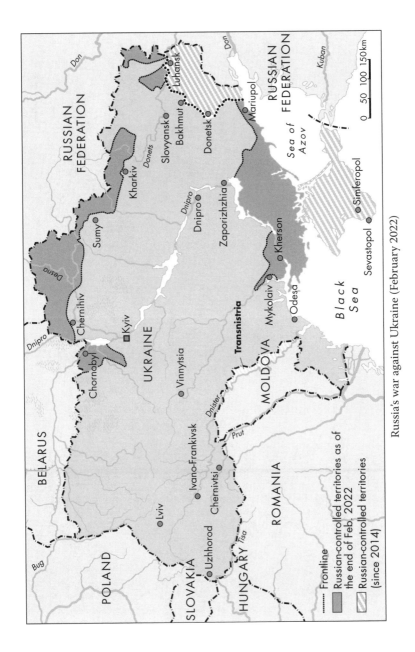

Russia's war against Ukraine (February 2022)

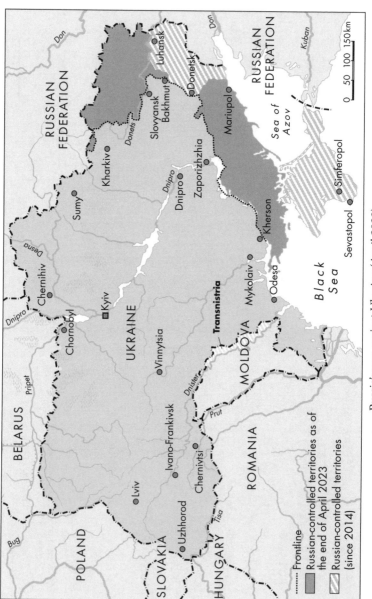

Russia's war against Ukraine (April 2023)

1

Why This War? Why Now?

March 7, 9:44 pm
[. . .]
These days, it is the individuals I encounter who
surprise and inspire me the most. Patrol officers and
women volunteers, priests and drivers, special forces
operators and villagers carrying hunting rifles. Beyond
this, a deep, clear outline takes shape, an outline of a
people that has finally recognized its own strength, the
strength of its rage as well as the strength of its unity.
Not an electorate divided among politicians, but a society
politicians have – finally – started speaking to openly
and honestly. It's crucial to acknowledge the trust and respect
we have for each other at this particular moment
so that we can hold on to it after we win. (. . .)
Serhiy Zhadan, Sky Above Kharkiv (2022).

The spectre of war has returned to Europe. This reality marks
a critical juncture in European (and global) politics and public
perceptions. Fourteen months after the start of Russia's full-
scale invasion of Ukraine on 24 February 2022, over 200,000
lives may have been lost on both sides – more precise casualty

figures are not yet available. According to UNHCR estimates, at least 15 million people have been displaced from or within Ukraine. This amounts to over a third of the Ukrainian population. The Ukrainian government currently estimates that this figure includes about 3 million Ukrainians (among them 300,000–700,000 children) who have been deported to Russia since the end of February 2022.

Over thirty years have passed since the end of the Soviet Union. Its disintegration has been significantly less peaceful than is often portrayed. Compared to the violent break-up of Yugoslavia, the wars over Nagorno-Karabakh, Transnistria, Abkhazia and South Ossetia seemed small from a West European perspective, although tens of thousands died and hundreds of thousands were displaced in these earlier wars. Similarly, the civil war in Tajikistan was generally overlooked in Europe. The two wars Russia fought in Chechnya in 1994–96 and 1999–2009 gained somewhat more coverage (several hundred thousands of people were killed, injured or displaced), but their origins in a national independence struggle and gradual transformation remained poorly understood, as Western governments supported the then Russian president Boris Yeltsin and chose by and large to ignore the second war under Vladimir Putin. Russia's warfare in Chechnya employed some of the brutal techniques later used in Syria and now in Ukraine. Like all of these wars, Russia's war against Ukraine is directly related to the disintegration of the USSR, which began long before its official end in December 1991, and which continues to have long-lasting repercussions.

Russia's war against Ukraine also ends the illusion of peaceful coexistence and a 'peace dividend' in Europe after the end of the Cold War. That illusion was not shaken by the wars in the former Yugoslavia in the early 1990s, nor even by the precursors of the current Russian invasion. Yet Russia's annexation of Crimea in 2014, combined with the Moscow-controlled war in parts of the Donbas region, led to some 14,000 deaths, about

1.5 million internally displaced individuals, and the flight of another 1 million to Russia. In the spring of 2021, Russia began to bolster its forces near Ukraine, stationing well over 100,000 soldiers on the Russian-Ukrainian and Belarusian-Ukrainian border.

Despite these preparations, the large-scale Russian attack on 24 February 2022 – which began with missile strikes on the capital Kyiv and major cities like Kharkiv, Odesa and Lviv, and saw Russian tanks advance into Ukraine from three sides – came as something of a surprise to many Western observers. In the EU, many had assumed that a rational cost-benefit calculation on Vladimir Putin's part would make a war of aggression of this kind unlikely. The populations in Western and Southern Europe were surprised most of all because Ukraine hardly existed on their mental maps. For them, Ukraine seemed very distant, and it has only become closer with the escalation of the war. Even the Ukrainian government had underestimated the risk of a large-scale attack, or at least played it down several times in public so as not to cause premature panic among the population and weaken the economy. The US intelligence community, however, had repeatedly warned of an escalation from late 2021.

This Europe-wide shock at the invasion on 24 February 2022 was quickly replaced by another widely unexpected realization: the strength of Ukraine's military and civilian resistance against the aggressor. In the case of an escalation, Western defence ministries and intelligence services had predicted a short war resulting in a Russian victory, based on calculations about the huge military imbalance in Russia's favour. Resistance is difficult to predict before the extreme case occurs, but it also requires a deeper understanding of society. According to an opinion poll conducted by the Kyiv International Institute of Sociology (KIIS) in December 2021, over half the Ukrainian population (excluding those in Crimea and the areas of Donbas not controlled by Kyiv) stated that they were ready to resist in the event of a new attack by Russia: 33 per cent expressed their willingness to engage in armed resistance and 22 per cent in civil resistance (multiple answers were possible). Overall, according to this survey, the will to resist was somewhat stronger in the west of the country than in the south and east. By the beginning of February 2022, this trend had further strengthened: across the country almost 58 per cent voiced their willingness to resist, including 37 per cent considering armed resistance and 25 per cent civil resistance. These polls demonstrate that Ukraine's morale and will to resist, already high, were only increasing in the run up to the invasion.

Since the first days of the war, during which the widely unexpected strength of Ukraine became visible, it has repeatedly been claimed that the Ukrainian nation is being built before our eyes at this very moment. This apparent unity does not correspond to the widespread image of the last twenty years or more of a Ukraine divided into east and west, along the fissures of language, ethnicity and region. However, the current resistance and civic engagement – from enrolling in the army and territorial defence units to organizing humanitarian aid, crowdfunding for army supplies and the reconstruction of infrastructure – is the consequence of a strong and pre-existing Ukrainian national identity rather than the cause of a Ukrainian identity in the making. This is an identity that, despite the country's internal diversity, is linked to a common understanding of what it means to be a Ukrainian citizen. One objective of this book is to correct the widespread flawed image of Ukraine before 24 February 2022 and to scrutinize further the reasons for this distorted perception.

Notwithstanding the shock felt by many in the West, the war did not begin unexpectedly. Wars have a history. They are about decisions at certain junctures and roads taken and not taken. Looked at over a longer period of time, patterns emerge that made a war in Ukraine – and a war of these huge dimensions – more likely. However, while it is important to understand the war in its context, we should not present it as an inevitable consequence of certain events and developments. History and politics are never without alternatives, even if with the benefit of hindsight the number of those claiming to have always predicted the war as it unfolded is growing. Such sweeping statements cannot do justice to the complexity of the preceding political process with its critical moments, misjudgements and decisions. In his speech on 21 February 2022, Putin stated his intentions in no uncertain terms. Three days later, the full-scale invasion began. Putin's central role is obvious. But the war cannot be narrowed down to his personality. The term 'Putin's war' does not sufficiently capture the reasons for it, even if he issued the orders. There is no one single cause that explains the descent into all-out war, but rather a series of interconnected developments that created the necessary if not sufficient conditions for this descent:

- the strengthening of Russia's authoritarian system including its revitalized neo-imperial claims
- the penetration of Russian society with state-sponsored memory politics and propaganda
- the democratization and westward orientation of Ukraine
- the strengthening of a civic Ukrainian identity
- the increasing discrepancy between Western and Russian security perceptions
- the growing contradictions in Western policies towards Russia
- Russia's gradual escalation of the war since 2014

Only in their interplay did these dynamics make Russia's war against Ukraine possible, even if Putin was the catalyst that turned this possibility into reality. Each of the listed developments links structural factors to political or societal actors. Thus, it is not a list of structural background factors. Included in the list are two developments related to Russia and Ukraine, two trends characterizing the relationship between Russia and the West, and a logic inherent in the war itself. Some of the developments might be subsumed under others, or they could be further subdivided, but they map the range of the central systemic, ideational, social and political developments that took on causal significance. The weighting of the various developments may vary. In my view, the interaction between the first and the third developments listed above plays the central role – as an explanation for both the increasing likelihood of war and for the unfolding dynamics of the war. The second and fourth developments in the list concern the state and societal mechanisms supporting the contrasting domestic and foreign policy models pursued by Russia and Ukraine. A democratic Ukraine integrated into Western institutions poses a threat to the authoritarian system in Russia. On the one hand, Ukraine undermines Russia's regional – and indirectly also its global – claim to power, which represents an important basis of legitimacy for Russia's authoritarian system. On the other hand, the path chosen by Ukraine also contains risks for the political system in Russia: it could contribute to the crystallization of hopes and expectations within Russian society or among the elites who might one day question the existing model from within.

The core issue is the self-preservation of Russia's authoritarian system, including its pretensions for neo-imperial power projection. The willingness to go to war to preserve this system underlines the perceived urgency within the Putin leadership of the danger posed by Ukraine to Russia. This is the context in which Putin as the key actor sought to use different windows of opportunity: giving the order first for the annexation of Crimea, then for the war in Donbas, and finally for the invasion of the whole of Ukraine.

The strengthening of Russia's authoritarian system including its revitalized neo-imperial claims

Putin's inauguration as president of the Russian Federation in May 2000 marked the start of the systematic establishment of an authoritarian system. His predecessor Boris Yeltsin had appointed him prime minister, and in this capacity Putin had overseen government affairs after Yeltsin's resignation at the end of 1999 until the presidential elections in March 2000. Yeltsin had pursued an ambivalent course between economic liberalization, democratization, violence and authoritarianism following the collapse of the Soviet Union. He had played a leading role in accelerating that collapse. His presidency is associated in particular with the 1993 constitution of the Russian Federation, which established a strong presidential system with decree powers. Yeltsin tolerated the far-reaching political influence of the economic oligarchs who profited from privatization, and he launched the first Chechen war of 1994–96. Putin was recruited from Russia's intelligence community as Yeltsin's hand-picked successor; his assumption of the presidency was accompanied by the second and even more brutal Chechen war in response to alleged Chechen terrorist attacks in Moscow and other Russian cities. Through repression and a centralizing restructuring of state power, the influence of the oligarchs on Russian political decision-making processes was reversed. The system relied more and more on the so-called 'power ministries' (the security apparatus and the military). The centralization and personalization of the system went hand in hand with ever more comprehensive control of the media, repression of any form of political opposition, and an increasing atomization of society. The Russian case therefore demonstrates that authoritarianism does not describe a static system, but one that makes adjustments and uses various incentives, means of pressure and delegations of responsibility to do so. Among the feedback mechanisms that sustain the political system is the close link between Russia's domestic and foreign policies: foreign policy is always also domestic policy and thus is an important factor for internal legitimacy; vice versa, domestic policy defines the scope of foreign policy and gives it social backing. Under Putin, external neo-imperialism has become fused with internal authoritarianism. The systematic expansion of the authoritarian system has included the explicit formulation and partial implementation of regional and global claims to power through war, for example in Georgia from 2008 and in Ukraine from 2014. The neo-imperial state ideology of Russia was decisively shaped by Putin himself. His proclaimed motivation for war is derived from it, and the preservation of the current authoritarian system depends on it.

The dictum that democracies do not wage war against each other has been empirically confirmed, but not the thesis that autocracies wage war more frequently than democracies. Even if the political nature of the system does not per se determine the outcome, the concentration of power in an authoritarian system plays a role in the ultimate decision on war and peace and its justification. There are fewer institutionally anchored hurdles on the way to ordering war, and hardly any elite or mass opposition to its ideological or material justification.

The penetration of Russian society with state-sponsored memory politics and propaganda

For years, the Russian state has been pursuing an extremely proactive policy of revising history in an attempt to provide moments for individual and collective identification and to legitimize the political system from within. The instrumentalization of history, from which political claims about the present and future are derived, is one of the central mechanisms of authoritarianism under Putin. As it was in the Soviet era, the victory over Nazi Germany is placed at the centre of historical memory directed from above. Victory Day on 9 May is the pivotal symbolic date for the Russian state. History has been made a central part of the neo-imperial state ideology in the system's everyday social life – through the rewriting and standardization of textbooks, the adaptation of historical research to the needs of the state, and continuous dissemination through the state media.

The emphasis is on continuities throughout Russian and Soviet history, while political upheavals such as the October Revolution and the collapse of the Soviet Union appear as aberrations in the official historiography. The neo-imperial claims to power have culminated in Putin's elaborations on Ukraine, which is denied its existence as an independent nation and state, and becomes a subordinate adjunct of Russia. Putin's concern for his own legacy is also reflected in the historical discourses he has engaged in personally and that have been constant reference points in the Russian media and beyond. In his various speeches, he has presented himself as the direct successor of the Russian tsars, especially Peter the Great, who modernized and expanded the Russian Empire by defeating internal and foreign enemies. Like other legacies, claims to power derived from history do not automatically unfold their political effect. They have to be activated. This can happen through friction with contrary political ideas – as happened in Ukraine.

The democratization and westward orientation of Ukraine

In the more than thirty years since Ukrainian independence, Ukraine has undergone a transformation into a political system that represents a clear alternative to the contemporary Russian-style authoritarianism. The transition has not always been straightforward and is not yet complete, but the fundamental course has been set by repeated social mobilization for independence, democracy and the rule of law. Cycles of mass protest have shaped the expectations and hopes of Ukrainians and created a new basis for civic and political engagement. Of particular importance were the 'Orange Revolution' of 2004, a mass protest which erupted over rigged presidential elections and helped to bring an opposition candidate to power, and the 'Euromaidan' of 2013–14, a mass protest against an unpopular president who at the last moment decided not to sign an Association Agreement with the EU (for further discussion, see Chapter 3). The comprehensive decentralization reform since 2014 has reinforced this trend at the local level in the sense that there is now more space for democratization from below. The democratization of Ukraine has been linked to a gradual orientation towards the West. Closer relations with the EU and NATO became official policy from 2004; after a renewed phase of foreign policy ambivalence from 2010 to 2013, integration with the EU and NATO have become government policy and a political consensus since the Euromaidan. In addition to this fundamental political decision, the societal orientation towards the West was also a logical consequence of the values and living standards demanded by the protest movements. The desire for integration into the EU became the majority opinion throughout the country. Support for NATO integration also grew from 2014, most notably in the south-east of the country, though overall it remained somewhat lower than the pro-EU consensus.

The strengthening of a civic Ukrainian identity

The transformation in Ukraine has strengthened a civic national identity linked to the Ukrainian state and political system. Numerous surveys by different agencies have tracked this trend, which intensified in the aftermath of the

Euromaidan, the annexation of Crimea, and during the war in Donbas. This identity emphasizes the principle of citizenship and is thus more inclusive than ethnic, linguistic, regional or other social identities. The recurring protest cycles in Ukraine were inclusive in their demands and mobilization strategies, and referred explicitly to general democratic principles and universal human rights. They contributed to the state-wide, society-centred self-definition of a polity that also played a central role in Zelensky's successful presidential election campaign in 2019. This civic identity has proven to be an important resource in times of crisis.

High levels of voluntary social engagement could be quickly redirected during the war into humanitarian aid (e.g. for the displaced), support for the army (e.g. in the form of donations or membership in territorial defence units), the preservation of local self-government structures and the ongoing reconstruction of infrastructure. The cumulative historical experience of sacrifice, discrimination and repression in the Russian and Soviet imperial contexts – which have played a more visible role in public discourse in Ukraine since the Orange Revolution (especially with reference to the Holodomor, the famine artificially created by Stalin) – lends a particular emotional intensity to the country's transformation into a political alternative to Russia. This historical experience and its reappraisal could, in theory, have promoted a narrower definition of an ethnic Ukrainian identity. However, with the decision to grant Ukrainian citizenship to all residents in 1991, the emphasis since independence has been on an inclusive state identity.

The increasing discrepancy between Western and Russian security perceptions

The motive for war singled out by Putin in his speeches is rooted in his perception of a threat to Russia emanating from the policies of the West, in particular NATO's eastward enlargement and, more specifically, the potential NATO integration of Ukraine (and Georgia). Even if Putin has never explicitly named the EU as a security risk, Ukraine's partial integration into the EU's internal market via an Association Agreement and a Deep and Comprehensive Free Trade Agreement, and, above all, the prospect of Ukraine's EU accession, also pose a political and economic risk for Russia. Integration into EU structures and practices underlines the fact that Ukraine embodies a political model that could also become more attractive in the future in Russia at the level of elites and society. Moreover, it reduces the attractiveness of the Russia-led Eurasian Economic Union. Putin generally does not think much of the EU and thus denies its relevance. He exploits its internal weaknesses and relies on bilateral relations with individual EU member states. Only weeks after the start of Russia's full-scale invasion, Ukraine submitted its application for EU membership and – within months – was offered a candidate status (together with Moldova). Russia's war has thus reinforced Ukraine's political choice and led all EU member states to endorse it.

Putin knew very well that NATO membership for Ukraine (and Georgia) – promised in principle, but without a road map, at the NATO Bucharest Summit in 2008 – was not on the agenda for the foreseeable future. The fact that he did not take up the offer made by Zelensky in the first days of the war to negotiate Ukraine's neutrality in exchange for reliable security guarantees shows that Putin is concerned with more than Ukraine's relationship with NATO. Nor did Putin engage in a substantive security dialogue with the United States and NATO, which was offered in the run-up to the escalation of the war in early 2022. Instead, he formulated maximum demands the result of which would have been a return to the status quo in Europe in the early 1990s, before the NATO-Russia Founding Act of 1997 and the subsequent eastward enlargement of NATO. He showed no interest in negotiations.

Russia's mantra that NATO promised not to expand eastwards in the context of German reunification is easily cleared up: there was no binding written agreement, though some of the political and diplomatic actors present during the negotiations did reassure their Soviet interlocutors at the time. Most importantly, the disintegration of the Warsaw Pact and the Soviet Union and the possibility of Central and East European states pushing for NATO membership were not yet on the horizon for those present.

Since the end of the Cold War, it has not proven possible to establish a European or international security architecture capable of integrating the different perceptions and interests. The political will to do so was initially weak in the Central and East European states – who felt that their security could only be guaranteed by NATO and, in particular, the United States – and then also in Russia and in the West. The intention mentioned in the NATO-Russia Founding Act to strengthen disarmament by adapting the 1990 Treaty on Conventional Armed Forces in Europe failed due to both Russian and NATO reservations. The expiry of or withdrawal from arms control treaties between the United States and Russia, as well as the nuclear rearmament of Russia and new global players such as China and India, have increased the general uncertainty at the international level.

The growing contradictions in Western policies towards Russia

The contradictions in Western policies towards Russia, and the lack of a coherent policy within the EU and NATO, had become increasingly obvious over time. Germany's approach became the clearest example of the contradictions inherent in the combination of dialogue and sanctions. On the one hand, Germany was one of the drivers behind the first EU sanctions in response to Russia's annexation of Crimea and the war in Donbas, as well as the regular extensions of those sanctions. On the other hand, there was much talk, especially in Germany, of channels for dialogue having to remain open – although in reality there was hardly any real dialogue and contacts broke off at many levels. Ultimately, the internal logic of authoritarianism in Russia was underestimated by many EU member states, Putin's neo-imperial claims were misunderstood as negotiable security interests, and the United States was premature in its downgrading of Russia's importance in comparison to the strategic economic cooperation and then political confrontation with China.

After 2014, despite EU and US sanctions and Russian countersanctions, Russia's prestige gas pipeline projects, Nord Stream 1 and 2, were deliberately pushed forward in Germany under the euphemistic description of 'change through trade' (*Wandel durch Handel*). The high energy-dependence of Germany – and of other EU states such as Austria, Italy and Hungary – on Russia was accepted nationally and at the EU level despite the growing political and economic confrontation. The associated security concerns of the Central and East European states, above all Ukraine, were not taken seriously enough. At the same time, disagreements within NATO and the EU were clearly visible, while the transatlantic Europe-US axis and the cohesion of NATO became increasingly fragile under US President Donald Trump. The contradictions in Western policies towards Russia as well as the apparent internal weaknesses of leading Western institutions left Russia with greater room for regional manoeuvre.

Russia's gradual escalation of the war since 2014

The fact that Russia gradually widened the war against Ukraine from the annexation of Crimea in 2014 to the war in Donbas and finally to the large-scale invasion of February 2022 allowed the Russian leadership to test its foreign policy leeway vis-à-vis the West, to give itself time for necessary adaptations in response to several rounds of Western sanctions, and to build support among its own population, or at least create a kind of war normality that was hardly questioned publicly. The phased expansion of the war from 2014 onwards also led to certain habituation effects in the EU, the West in general, and even in Ukraine.

It was against the backdrop of these seven interacting dynamics that, on Putin's orders, the full-scale invasion of Ukraine began in the early hours of 24 February 2022. After months of a massive troop build up close to the Ukrainian border, Russian forces attacked Ukraine from the north, east and south simultaneously. The capital Kyiv immediately came under fire as one of the main targets, as did the city of Kharkiv in the east and cities in central and western Ukraine. The 24th of February 2022 marks a turning point in European history. The reference to this date as the 'start of the war', which has dominated international discourse since then, is inaccurate, however, because Russia had already been at war in Ukraine since 2014. Terminology defines the framework of what can be said and imagined. Widely used terms such as 'the Ukraine conflict' or 'the Ukraine crisis' are equally problematic. It is no coincidence that the term 'Ukraine crisis' also plays a prominent role in Russian discourse, as it suggests that Ukraine is unable to overcome its internal problems, while Russia appears uninvolved. The term 'civil war', which is frequently used in Russia, is even more of a distortion, as it portrays the war in Donbas as a conflict within Ukraine fought by Ukrainians. This term sometimes reverberates through Western public discourse. Russian disinformation and Western disinterest tend to reinforce each other. The term 'the Ukraine war', which is frequently used in the Western media at present, also draws attention to a war in Ukraine which, without any reference to Russia, can be misunderstood as an internal or civil war or as a war Ukraine is responsible for. A clear designation is therefore essential: Russia is waging war against Ukraine.

The problem with the word 'conflict' is more complicated. It sounds less drastic than 'war' and conveys the image of a smaller or smouldering conflict the escalation of which might be prevented or at least contained by certain regulatory measures. The common designation of the war in Donbas as a 'conflict' has contributed to this perception. However, sometimes the term 'Ukraine conflict' has been used to refer to the larger international context that lies behind the annexation of Crimea and the war in Donbas, i.e. it then extends beyond the actual war to questions of international cooperation and confrontation.

In the social sciences there is a field defined as 'conflict research', sometimes also described as 'peace and conflict research', which deals with the whole range from large-scale wars to latent conflict potentials, conflict prevention and efforts to maintain peace. It is part of the responsibility of academia to be aware of the pitfalls inherent in the popular use of these terms, to critically question the term 'conflict' in public discourse, and not to use it if it obscures political reality.

Moreover, war directs the attention of politics and the wider public towards military capacities and strategies. By comparison, empirical research on social and political developments before, during and after a war may appear as 'soft' and secondary. Russia's war against Ukraine, however, clearly shows that identities, transformation processes, the rewriting of history, and authoritarian state discourses are not of secondary importance but play an absolutely central role, including in the decision about war and peace.

Ukraine

2

Independence and Territory

The history of Ukraine has been significantly shaped by various empires: the Polish-Lithuanian Commonwealth and the Habsburg Empire in the west, the Crimean Khanate and the Ottoman Empire in the south, the Russian Empire in the south, the north-east and in parts of central Ukraine, and the Soviet Union on the entire territory of Ukraine. In 1991, Ukraine became an independent country within the Soviet-era borders of the Ukrainian Soviet Socialist Republic (Ukrainian SSR). The various empires have left structural and cultural legacies. The traces of previous empires partly re-emerge beside the Soviet legacies. The history of Ukraine is best understood as an entangled transregional history.

The idea of the Ukrainian nation was formulated in the nineteenth century by transnationally active cultural elites around Kharkiv University in eastern Ukraine, a region which at that time was part of the Russian Empire. Western Ukraine, then part of the Habsburg Empire, ultimately offered a more open political environment for the development of this idea. In the early twentieth century, western Ukraine – in interaction with the Ukrainian diaspora in North America, which began to formulate its national identity through the experience of

emigration – became the core of the independence movement. At first, it evolved within the Habsburg Empire; around
the end of the First World War it crystallized in the short-lived
Ukrainian People's Republic. During the Soviet Union the idea
of Ukrainian independence remained most closely associated with the dissident movement concentrated in western
Ukraine.

In its focus on the pursuit of independence, Ukrainian historiography does not differ significantly from other national
historiographies. State independence gives historiography a
supposedly clear point of reference, but this ultimately says
little about contemporary statehood within its internationally
recognized borders. In Ukrainian historiography, the quest for
independence tends to be recounted in a rather linear manner
from the Middle Ages to the present day. The medieval empire
of Kyivan Rus (the beginnings of which date back to the ninth
century and are claimed by both Ukraine and Russia as the
cradle of their respective statehoods and cultures), the Cossack
state (Hetmanate) of the seventeenth century and the Ukrainian
People's Republic of 1918–20 are the most important points of
reference in this historical line that leads up to 1991.

In the context of the First World War and the October
Revolution there were brief periods of Ukrainian autonomy
or independence between 1917 and 1920, first as part of the
policies of Germany and the Habsburg Empire, and then in
different configurations during the civil war that followed the
October Revolution. The Ukrainian People's Republic existed
from January 1918 until its capture by the Red Army in February
1920, after which it was integrated into the Soviet Union as
the Ukrainian SSR in 1922. Following this brief experience of
statehood, Lenin's nationality policy in the early Soviet period
further strengthened Ukrainian national identity both through
the promotion of the Ukrainian language and culture and
through the administrative separation of the Ukrainian and
Russian Soviet republics.

For Ukraine, the Stalin era is inextricably linked to the intraparty Stalinist terror and the great, man-made famine (Holodomor) of 1932–33, which killed at least 3 to 4 million people (some estimates are much higher). Here, Stalin's policy of collectivization coincided with his aim of breaking the Ukrainian national movement. The recognition of the Holodomor as a genocide has been a central part of Ukrainian remembrance and political life since the Orange Revolution in 2004.

The Second World War was another deep trauma for Ukraine. Under Nazi and Soviet rule, the number of victims in the region between central Poland and western Russia – which includes Ukraine, Belarus and the Baltic states and was called the 'Bloodlands' by historian Timothy Snyder – is estimated at 14 million people. The general West European understanding of twentieth-century history has still not come to terms with the fact that the Holocaust also took place outside of Germany and Poland, or that the Soviet war victims were not 'only' Russians.

Experiences of collective suffering, repression and Russification marked Soviet Ukrainian history. Along with these lingering traumas, the imperial legacy of the Soviet Union also includes the at least intermittent promotion or toleration of the Ukrainian language and culture. Ukraine was nominally a 'sovereign' Soviet Union Republic, even a member state of the United Nations, but this was on paper only. As mentioned above, Ukraine became independent at the end of 1991 within its Soviet-era borders. Its western border is the result of Soviet border demarcation after the end of the Second World War; its southern border took on its present form with the administrative transfer of Crimea in 1954 from the Russian Soviet Federative Socialist Republic (RSFSR) to the Ukrainian Soviet Socialist Republic. Ukraine's eastern border – a more than 2,000-kilometre-long border with Russia – dates back to the negotiations within the Communist Party of the Soviet Union in the 1920s in connection with the establishment of the Soviet Union. This border appeared to be the least controversial at the time of the disintegration of the Soviet Union in 1991.

The Ukrainian declaration of independence, passed by the parliament of the Ukrainian SSR after the August coup in 1991 and legitimated via a referendum on 1 December the same year, sealed the end of the Soviet Union and created a strong basis for an independent Ukraine. In that referendum, over 90 per cent of the voting population (on a turnout of about 84 per cent) came out in favour of state independence, including a majority of 54 per cent in Crimea and 57 per cent in Sevastopol, a city which had special military-administrative status in the Soviet Union. In the eastern and southern regions, such as Donetsk, Kharkiv and Odesa, the vote in favour of independence was as high as 80 to 90 per cent. The referendum mobilized Ukrainian society around support for the idea of independence. There were regional differences in the turnout: in Crimea it was slightly below 68 per cent (in Sevastopol just below 64 per cent), in Odesa, Kharkiv, Donetsk and Luhansk 75–80 per cent, i.e., even in the south-east of the country a considerable majority participated in the referendum and voted for this fundamental step.

The question of independence has stayed with Ukraine and with external observers beyond 1991. With the Budapest Memorandum of 1994, Russia, the United States and the United Kingdom guaranteed Ukraine's state sovereignty and territorial integrity within the borders of 1991 in return for Ukraine's accession to the Nuclear Non-Proliferation Treaty and the transfer of the Soviet-era nuclear weapons stationed in Ukraine to Russia. Similar memorandums were concluded with Belarus and Kazakhstan. For Ukraine, this agreement was a critical internationally guaranteed pillar of its future security, even if its legal status remained ambiguous. In 2014 the Memorandum became obsolete when Russia undermined Ukraine's territorial integrity by annexing Crimea and the guarantor states were unable or unwilling to do anything about it. The Budapest Memorandum contained no mechanism for handling a border dispute or an attack on Ukrainian territory.

The notion of independence continued to resonate in Ukrainian society beyond 1991, though its exact meaning seemed to vary over time. According to a survey by the Kyiv International Institute of Sociology (KIIS) in June 2021, just over 70 per cent of Ukrainians said they would have voted for independence, 8 per cent said they would have opposed it, and just under 22 per cent said they were unsure whether they would have taken part in this type of referendum. Converting these figures, about 78 per cent of the population would have taken part, and of these, just under 90 per cent would have voted in favour of independence and 10 per cent against. These figures correspond to those of the 1991 referendum. Asking the question about independence three decades after the dissolution of the Soviet Union does not mean the same thing as in 1991, as at that time the idea was associated with greater uncertainty. In the intervening years, the question may have become more of a gauge of general satisfaction or dissatisfaction with the government's performance since the early 1990s. According to the entire KIIS survey series on the question, approval ratings for independence were lower in the period between the Orange Revolution and the Euromaidan. In retrospect, however, the results show, above all, how high the approval for independence was already in 1991.

The most serious internal territorial challenge for the newly independent Ukraine after 1991 was the political integration of the Crimean peninsula. Crimea was the only Ukrainian region to be granted an autonomy status. This process started at the beginning of 1991, when Ukraine was still part of the disintegrating Soviet Union. In many parts of the USSR, formally existing autonomy rights became the basis of political claims; in some places, regional autonomies were questioned or abolished in the context of national movements at the level of the Soviet republics. This led to counter-mobilization and violence, for example in Abkhazia and South Ossetia. An autonomy movement in Crimea wanted to secure the region's status as an Autonomous Soviet Socialist Republic (ASSR) under direct Soviet jurisdiction. In January 1991, a referendum in Crimea with a turnout of just over 81 per cent resulted in a majority of over 90 per cent of those taking part voting in favour of an ASSR within the USSR. Instead, the Supreme Soviet of the Ukrainian SSR decided in February 1991 to contain the mobilization for regional autonomy by creating an ASSR within the Ukrainian SSR, which was more typical of the Soviet administrative order. This compromise proved to be short-lived, as the Soviet Union was dissolved a few months later.

Nevertheless, the poorly defined institutional framework of the autonomy provided a starting point for the negotiations about the status of Crimea within independent Ukraine. The principle of autonomy is not as clearly linked to conflict and violence as is often claimed. In Crimea, the idea of autonomy has both crystallized conflict potential and opened up a framework for conflict management.

According to the last Soviet referendum in 1989, 67 per cent of the then total of 2.4 million Crimean inhabitants described their 'nationality' as Russian, 25.8 per cent as Ukrainian and 1.6 per cent as Crimean Tatar. In addition, there were numerous other minorities. The Crimean Tatar share of the population had declined gradually as a result of the settlement policies of the Russian Empire. At the end of the nineteenth century, their share of the Crimean population, according to official statistics, was still about one third, but by the beginning of the Second World War it had dropped to just under 20 per cent. The deportation of the entire Crimean Tatar population by Stalin in 1944 – on the pretext of their collaboration with German troops – and the subsequent settlement of Russians and Ukrainians in Crimea changed the ethnic composition dramatically. Only after the collapse of the Soviet Union did the Crimean Tatar share of the population rise again, to about 12 per cent, with a mass return to Crimea from the places of deportation in Central Asia and Russia.

In 1993, *The Economist* warned of a 'long-running, acrimonious, possibly bloody and conceivably nuclear dispute over Crimea' that could ignite over Crimea. This apocalyptic scenario was exaggerated already at the time of writing, but it illustrates that there was widespread fear of conflict after the end of the Soviet Union. The potential for conflict in Crimea in the early 1990s had several dimensions: the relations between the Ukrainian government, the regional political institutions in Simferopol and the separatist Russian movement; intraregional tensions arising from the mass return and unregulated settlement of the Crimean Tatars; and the bilateral relations between Ukraine and Russia. The latter were uneasy, given the reluctance of parts of the Russian elite to recognize Ukrainian independence, the difficult division of the Black Sea Fleet, the transfer of Soviet nuclear weapons stationed on the territory of Ukraine, and Ukraine's dependence on subsidized Russian energy supplies. In many dimensions, Crimea was of strategic and symbolic importance for Russia.

The confrontation between Kyiv and Simferopol deteriorated in the years 1992–95. In May 1992, the regional parliament declared an independent 'Crimean Republic'. The concept of independence remained ambiguous: the constitution adopted at the regional level continued to refer to Crimea as part of Ukraine, but at the same time tried to regulate relations between Kyiv and Simferopol as if they were two sovereign entities. A revised Crimean constitution, adopted in autumn 1992 in response to protest from the central government, referred to the 'Autonomous Republic of Crimea'. Nevertheless, Crimea had secured its own coat of arms and a tricolour flag resembling Russia's flag. In January 1994, Yurii Meshkov, one of the leaders of the broad-based Russian

movement consisting of various political and social organizations, was elected President of Crimea, a position created on
the basis of the new Crimean constitution. Under Meshkov's
leadership, the so-called 'Blok Rossiya' won a majority (fifty-
four out of ninety-eight seats) in the regional parliamentary
elections in March–April 1994. A new referendum on greater
regional autonomy followed in May. With it, the Crimean
constitution of May 1992, the most far-reaching in its claim
to independence, was reinstated. The Ukrainian government
declared the referendum invalid. Under pressure, the Crimean
parliament rescinded its decision in June 1994.

From the summer of 1994 onwards, Crimean politics became
highly fractious. Political disputes between President Meshkov
and the Crimean parliament intensified. Meshkov appealed to
Russian President Boris Yeltsin and nationalist Russian MPs
for help to establish closer ties. He even temporarily moved
Crimea into the Moscow time zone. However, the separatist
pro-Russian movement began to disintegrate due to internal
disagreements.

In September 1994, the new Ukrainian president Leonid
Kuchma managed to install a loyal head of government in
Crimea, Anatolii Franchuk. In March 1995, Kyiv finally gained
the upper hand. The Ukrainian parliament officially repealed
the Crimean constitution of 1992 as well as a number of regionally enacted laws and decrees, removed Meshkov as president
and abolished the Crimean presidency altogether. There was
no local resistance, and Meshkov was forced to leave Crimea.
By decree, President Kuchma placed Crimea under the direct
control of the Ukrainian presidential administration.

Overall, four factors contributed to defusing the conflict
potential associated with Crimea in the 1990s:

- Crimea's multi-ethnicity
- the internal weakness and factionalism of the regional
  Russian movement

- Kyiv's policy of avoiding escalation
- the lack of active support from Russia under Yeltsin

In retrospect, the last point was the decisive one, even though all four factors were closely interlinked. Against the background of these factors, a particular political dynamic gained significance: the parallel processes of constitution-making at the national and regional levels. Even if the regional pro-Russian forces failed in their attempts to expand their political power through a series of Crimean constitutions, they contributed to constitutional negotiations becoming the main instrument of conflict management. In the end, the 1996 Ukrainian constitution defined Ukraine as a unitary state with twenty-seven administrative units, including twenty-four *oblasti*, two cities with special status (Kyiv and Sevastopol) and the Autonomous Republic of Crimea. The Ukrainian government under President Kuchma thus showed the necessary flexibility to anchor Crimean autonomy within the Ukrainian constitution, even though it contradicted the definition of Ukraine as a unitary state. The Crimean constitution of 1998 then defined the scope of Crimean autonomy, which, although weak in content, went beyond a mere symbolic function, for example in the guarantees for the use of Russian and Crimean Tatar in addition to the state language Ukrainian – which was unique among Ukraine's regions – and the possibility of retaining tax revenues levied in the region.

In the 1990s Crimea's multi-ethnicity and the Russian language shared in everyday life helped to prevent a deep ethno-political polarization of society and the elites. The dominance of the Russian language in Crimea is the result of imperial Russian and Soviet settlement and cultural policies. Both the quarter of the Crimean population that defined itself as 'Ukrainian' in the 1989 and 2001 official censuses and the Crimean Tatars returning from 1991 from Central Asia and Russia were mostly Russian-speakers. Stalin's deportation of the Crimean Tatars had been accompanied by extensive Russification, even if the deportees and their descendants had retained their identification with the Crimean Tatar language and relearned it after their return to Crimea. After independence, the Ukrainian government gave Ukrainian the constitutional status of sole state language, but refrained from overregulating the use of Russian. Overall, Kyiv adopted a pragmatic attitude towards the region and, despite some tense moments, signalled interest in a peaceful political negotiation of the institutional relationship between Kyiv and Simferopol. Moreover, the Russian movement in Crimea proved weak and quickly discredited itself in the eyes of the regional population – not least through its economic incompetence – in the crisis years of the early 1990s. Yeltsin did not support the pro-Russian movement in Crimea and thus recognized that Crimea was a part of Ukraine. Individual Russian politicians, including nationalists such as Vladimir Zhirinovsky and Moscow mayor Yurii Luzhkov, had vocally supported Crimean separatism, but their positions did not become government policy. Given that Yeltsin had himself supported the aspirations for sovereignty at the level of the Soviet republics, including the RSFSR, he was neither able nor willing to challenge the borders of newly independent Ukraine. He was also distracted by domestic political disputes over Russia's own constitution-making. Russia was deeply divided over the course of economic reform, which brought Yeltsin into violent confrontation with parliament and a complex process of negotiation over relations between Moscow and the subjects of the Russian Federation with their differing political, economic and cultural aspirations. The first Chechen war, starting in late 1994, consumed much of Yeltsin's attention and was at the same time a deterrent for Kyiv and Simferopol not to exacerbate the crisis in their relations. Russia was the official successor state of the Soviet Union, but it had not yet consolidated its new international role. It was economically weak and not yet capable of a new projection of its military or political strength.

Yeltsin prioritized good bilateral relations with Ukraine. This included the peaceful transfer of Soviet nuclear weapons located on Ukrainian territory in return for guarantees of Ukraine's sovereignty (as discussed above). In 1992, both President Leonid Kravchuk and Yeltsin had attempted to unilaterally assume command of the Black Sea Fleet by decree, but then agreed on a dual supreme command until a final agreed division. In practice, this led to a division according to Russian and Ukrainian oaths of office respectively and entailed the possibility of a confrontation. Ultimately, half of the fleet and its facilities were to go to Ukraine and half to Russia; Ukraine successively 'sold' parts of its half to Russia in exchange for subsidized energy supplies. Russia also secured from Ukraine the right to rent a military base in Sevastopol.

In parallel to the internal Ukrainian constitutional process, numerous rounds of Russian-Ukrainian negotiations took place to regulate the division of the Black Sea Fleet and define the overarching framework of bilateral relations. In 1997, the long-negotiated Treaty of Friendship, Cooperation and Partnership, also known as the 'Great Treaty', was signed by Kuchma and Yeltsin in Kyiv. It came into force in 1999 after a delayed ratification by the Russian parliament. The treaty was initially valid for twenty years, with an in-built renewal option. With this treaty, both sides again mutually recognized their territorial integrity – which was reaffirmed in 2003 in a bilateral border treaty and an agreement on the joint use of the Sea of Azov – and formulated declarations of intent with regard to their cooperation on matters ranging from security policy to cultural issues. Russia agreed to pay rent for its naval base in Sevastopol, which was offset repeatedly against Ukrainian gas debts. In 2010, the contractual agreement on Russia's use of the base was renegotiated and extended until 2042 in exchange for discounted gas supplies. This was politically controversial in Ukraine, as the Ukrainian executive had deliberately limited the discussion before the extension of the contract. For various factions in parliament and for parts of society this renewal went too far in the direction of a permanent stationing of foreign troops on Ukrainian territory.

Even if the potential for conflict over the Black Sea Fleet and the institutional status of Crimea had been managed relatively successfully in the 1990s, other challenges remained, in particular the integration of the Crimean Tatars and the economic development of the peninsula. Politically, the region quickly became an integral part of south-eastern Ukraine from 1998 onwards. The Crimean population regularly participated in regional and national elections and found itself aligning with the movements and parties that dominated the south and east of the country. There were no new separatist movements in Crimea or eastern Ukraine before 2014, although this is presented differently in official Russian state rhetoric today.

The historically conditioned regional diversity is one of the main features of the Ukrainian state. It reflects numerous (post-)imperial linkages, for example at the level of economic relations or personal contacts. Ukraine's regional diversity and its political relevance have often been misunderstood. Where Ukraine was present in the Western public debate at all, it appeared as a country divided into east and west on the basis of ethnic or linguistic differences between 'Ukrainians' and 'Russians' or between Ukrainian-speakers and Russian-speakers. Overall, the regional differences – which go far beyond the division of the country into two parts, and the identities and interests associated with them – are more diffuse, more permeable and less conflictual in everyday life than is generally assumed from the outside.

Beyond the official administrative division of Ukraine into twenty-four regions (*oblasti*), the Autonomous Republic of Crimea and the cities of Kyiv and Sevastopol, different regional classifications have been used. A widespread standard is the division of the country into four macro-regions: west, central, south and east. Further distinctions within these macro-regions can be useful, e.g. between rural and urban or, more specifically, industrial locations in the south or east of the country. Depending on what issues are placed at the centre of the analysis, the northern regions have also played a visible role, although they have rarely been highlighted as a separate region.

Border regions within the macro-regions, or border regions connecting them, are characterized by their own dynamics. Ukraine's western and south-western borders are on the external border of the EU. Here, the EU regulates the mobility of the population. Compared to the situation before the EU's eastern enlargement, new restrictions have been imposed. In the south, the annexation of Crimea in 2014 has reduced the personal contacts between the population of Crimea and the neighbouring *oblasti* to a minimum.

Ukraine borders the de facto state of Transnistria, which, with Russia's support, opposed the Moldovan national movement in 1992. Since that violent confrontation, Transnistria has maintained a complex set of relations with both Russia and the rest of the Moldovan state. A small Russian military garrison has been stationed in Transnistria since the end of the Soviet Union. The border with Transnistria has been a problem for Ukraine mainly because of illegal trade, not because of a military threat. Against the background of the Russian war of aggression since February 2022, this constellation is changing. Russia could try to use Transnistria as a base or try to conquer a corridor through Ukraine linking Crimea to Transnistria.

In the east, the long Ukrainian-Russian border was permeable for a long time. With Russia's war in Donbas since 2014, it became a massive security risk for Ukraine and for Europe as a whole. The ceasefire line ('contact line') negotiated in the Minsk Protocol (2014) and Minsk II (2015) partitioned the Donbas effectively into two parts and blocked Ukraine's access to its actual state border in the east (for more information, see Chapter 6).

Regions are an important component part of Ukrainian politics, but the political preferences of the population are not predetermined by the ethnic, linguistic or socioeconomic characteristics of their regions. The degree of attitudinal diversity or unanimity across regions has varied depending on the context or issue area. In western Ukraine, parties and ideas associated with the Ukrainian national movement played an important role in the aftermath of the break-up of the Soviet Union, while in eastern Ukraine industrial structures and other socioeconomic factors shaped local identities, oligarchic politics and electoral outcomes. Regions in Ukraine do not function as monolithic actors, and the interests of political and economic elites usually vary both within and between regions.

Since Ukraine's independence, the voting behaviour of the population – with the exception of the 2019 presidential election, in which Volodymyr Zelensky emerged as the clear winner – had shown distinct regional patterns. These reflected different political preferences and societal concerns, for example with regard to political and economic reforms, or relations with NATO, the EU or the Russia-dominated Eurasian Economic Union (or earlier Russia-led economic integration projects). However, regional electoral differentiation was not limited to a single issue and did not challenge Ukrainian state independence. In 2004, in the repeat second round of the presidential elections, brought about by the mass protests of the 'Orange Revolution', the electoral east-west split was particularly apparent: sixteen contiguous *oblasti* in western and central Ukraine, including Kyiv, voted for the 'orange' opposition candidate Viktor Yushchenko, while eight neighbouring *oblasti* in the south-east and in Sevastopol voted for the 'blue' candidate Viktor Yanukovych, who was supported by the incumbent Kuchma as well as Moscow. Until 2019, the dominant parties in the south-east were conglomerates representing the economic interests of the most influential regional oligarchs. Before the Euromaidan protests in 2013–14, the predominant party in the south-east was the Party of Regions, which then transformed into the 'Opposition Bloc', from which, in turn, the 'Opposition Platform – For Life' split off as the dominant force.

These parties regularly argued for an official status for the Russian language at the regional or national level, and placed the socioeconomic concerns of the regional population at the heart of their campaigns. They cannot be adequately summed up in the term 'pro-Russian', although they are almost always described as such in the Western media. The adjective 'pro-Russian' overemphasizes issues of ethnic identity or language practice, although these identities played a secondary role in elections. Moreover, it wrongly equates these identities with disloyalty to the Ukrainian state. Especially since the war in Donbas, but also following the establishment of closer economic relations with the EU, some oligarchs with core interests in these regions have pragmatically oriented their business activities in different directions. Cultural issues, such as language policy, functioned primarily as political instruments at the disposal of competing interest groups.

The party spectrum in other regions remained more diverse and competitive than in the east and south of the country. Moreover, in local elections, the regional division had made way for a more colourful party-political picture, especially since 2015. Although the Opposition Bloc, or the 'Opposition Platform – For Life', remained the strongest force in many local constituencies in the south-east, parties traditionally based in western or central Ukraine often came a close second. This trend continued in the local elections of 2020 and – reinforced by the new incentives provided by Ukraine's decentralization reforms – brought about new interactions that were beginning to question the seemingly fixed regional dividing lines from below.

Even though the terms 'pro-Russian' and 'pro-Western' never adequately described the parties or presidential candidates, there have been regional differences in the foreign policy orientation of the most influential parties and their voters. These regional differences decreased over time. The Euromaidan, the subsequent political decision to make EU and NATO integration official state objectives, and Russia's war since 2014 have consolidated a broad consensus in support of EU and NATO accession.

By the end of 2019, according to a series of comparable opinion polls by different agencies, about 60 per cent of Ukrainians were in favour of joining the EU (during that year, support had increased by about 10 per cent). In the east and south of the country, support stood at 30 and 40 per cent respectively. By comparison, only about 10–15 per cent overall were positively disposed towards integration into the Eurasian Economic Union at the end of 2019 (at the beginning of that year it had been just below 25 per cent overall and about 35 per cent in the east and south). Shortly before Russia's full-scale attack on Ukraine in 2022, overall support for EU membership was as high as 67 per cent (KIIS December 2021). Even in the south-east, 54 per cent were in favour according to this survey, compared to 76 per cent in western and central Ukraine taken together. Closer ties with NATO have been a more controversial issue than closer relations with the EU. The alternative idea of a neutral Ukraine, however, has become increasingly unattractive in the midst of Russia's war of aggression. Since the start of the war in 2014, support for Ukraine's membership in NATO has increased significantly, especially in the south-east of the country. In Zelensky's home region of Dnipropetrovsk, the increase was particularly significant. At the end of December 2021, approval and rejection of NATO integration were balanced in the south-east at around 40 per cent, while approval in western Ukraine was as high as 70 per cent. Overall, around 59 per cent of the Ukrainian population took a position in favour of NATO integration at the end of 2021 (KIIS December 2021).

Even though issues such as the promotion of the Ukrainian language in schools and in everyday life, as well as the status of the Russian language, regularly played a role in presidential elections, each Ukrainian president ultimately had to balance the different interests and identities in the country as a whole. In this way, diversity can help to contain potentially destabilizing policies. For a long time, language use was not regulated by law beyond the constitutional anchoring of Ukrainian as the state language. In 2012, a language law was passed under President Yanukovych which created the possibility of giving a language a regional status if the minority speaking it accounted for more than 10 per cent of the regional population. Some regional and local councils made use of this option. In addition to the Russian language in south-eastern Ukraine, this regulation also applied to, for example, Hungarian, Moldovan and Romanian in the western border regions.

There were protests against the law, which was initially suspended after the Euromaidan but then reintroduced – only to be eventually overturned by the Constitutional Court in 2018. It was replaced in 2019 by a new language law drafted under post-Euromaidan president Petro Poroshenko. The law stipulated the use of the Ukrainian language in all state offices and in the public sector, including the education and health sectors. It also aimed to increase the presence of Ukrainian in the media, the book market, industry and the service sector, but without banning the use of Russian. The active promotion by law of the Ukrainian language in public and in the workplace occurred late and partially – contrary to Russian state rhetoric alleging systematic discrimination against Russians and Russian-speakers in Ukraine.

The 2019 presidential elections were the first national elections to generate a cross-regional electoral consensus. In the second round, Zelensky was able to achieve a clear majority against the incumbent Poroshenko – with one exception in Galicia in western Ukraine. Zelensky had deliberately avoided formulating a concrete election programme, but was able to read the mood in society better than his politically more experienced rival. He singled out the fight against corruption and an end to the war in Donbas as his primary goals. Zelensky, who comes from Kryvii Rih, a city in Dnipropetrovsk region, spoke almost exclusively Russian during the election campaign and explicitly addressed the linguistic, ethnic and regional diversity of Ukraine. His inclusive message was directed at all citizens, including those in Crimea and in the areas of the Donbas that were not under Kyiv's control at the time. The contrast to Poroshenko's election slogan 'Army, Language, Faith', projecting a narrower conception of Ukrainian identity, could not have been starker. Moreover, Poroshenko argued for severing economic and social ties with the non-government-controlled Donbas and Crimea.

Before being catapulted into national politics, Zelensky was known throughout the country for his TV series *Servant of the People*, in which he played a teacher who unexpectedly becomes president and fights against corruption by means of grassroots politics. Zelensky's lack of political experience has been highlighted many times by his domestic opponents and in international reporting. What has been underestimated, however, is his understanding of Ukrainian society, honed during his extensive travels up and down the country in his capacity as an actor, producer and co-owner of a production company. This bottom-up experience is an important part of his electoral success and later of his authenticity as the people's president in wartime who stayed in Kyiv and addresses his people and international audiences on a daily basis. His election as president in 2019 and the absolute majority for his new party 'Servant of the People' in the parliamentary elections that year highlighted not only the frustration of the population with slow reforms, corruption and war, but also a greater sense of unity around a civic Ukrainian identity.

The term 'national identity' may sound rather abstract. In the (post-)colonial view of Eastern Europe, it tends to be primarily associated with ethnic criteria. However, identities are not static phenomena. In practice, everyone has different overlapping identities at any one time. Depending on the context, one or more identities can be of greater importance to individuals or a community than others. For instance, the prioritization of a national identity in western Ukraine, e.g. in Galicia, has been the norm historically, whereas in the east, e.g. in the Donbas region, socioeconomic and regional identities were more salient. Over time, these identity dimensions were reordered. In the humanities and social sciences, the term 'national identity' is qualified by further distinguishing between ethnic and state-centred or 'civic' identities. A focus on ethnic criteria is essentially exclusive and defines cultural boundaries between individuals and groups, whereas an identity based on the polity and the civic principle of citizenship is a more inclusive notion that puts the emphasis on a political choice and participation. At the state level and at the level of individuals, identities can oscillate between the two poles. They are often ascribed from the outside, but are not easy to grasp empirically. People may not describe their identities in the terms used in academia. Opinion polls stylize identities and can divide respondents into artificial categories, especially if there are no options to indicate multiple identities, for example by ranking one's identities or allowing for categories that cover mixed identities.

The last official census in Ukraine (2001) still forced respondents to choose between Ukrainian and Russian 'nationality'. Many surveys today allow for more flexibility by adding mixed categories (e.g. 'both Russian and Ukrainian nationality', 'both Ukrainian and Russian as mother tongues'). The impression of a divided society can thus also be the result of dichotomizing categories used in survey research. In Soviet times, the term 'nationality' (*natsional'nist'*) was the category that denoted ethnic origin and was derived from the parents' identification. In the 2001 census, 77.8 per cent gave their nationality as Ukrainian and 17.3 per cent as Russian. Overall, 67.5 per cent named Ukrainian as their mother tongue and 29.6 per cent listed Russian. Compared to the last Soviet census of 1989, the trend already leaned towards the 'Ukrainian' identity categories. Over time, this trend has become even stronger, with only 10–20 per cent of Ukrainians naming Russian as their mother tongue in various surveys up until the end of 2021.

The term 'nationality' is still regularly used in surveys today, but the interpretation has become more ambiguous over time. We know from focus group discussions, individual interviews and survey experiments with different response categories that the meaning of 'nationality' has shifted and now combines ethnic and civic interpretations. Equating 'nationality' with ethnic identity is therefore problematic. The translation of the term *natsional'nist'* into English is also imprecise, as in English 'nationality' denotes citizenship. The lack of clearly delineated categories has a direct impact on our understanding of complex identities in Ukraine. The standard category 'mother tongue' is equally problematic. As survey research over time has shown, it is primarily a symbolic category rather than a description of actual language use. It is thus closely linked to the respondents' understanding of identity. In contrast to the earlier census categories, opinion polls have increasingly distinguished between mother tongue and everyday language practice, with answers to both questions allowing for bilingual response categories. Prior to 2022 surveys that allow for bilingual answers, about one fifth of the Ukrainian population identified Russian as their 'mother tongue' while choosing answers describing various forms of Russian-Ukrainian bilingualism in daily life. Here, a context-dependent range of passive to active bilingualism becomes tangible, which has hardly been perceived outside Ukraine and is not as conflictual in everyday life as is often assumed.

Moreover, a language identity or actual language use in public or private are not necessarily congruent with ethnic criteria. Over the three decades of independence, a new younger generation has been socialized into the Ukrainian language, without the Russian language being displaced from everyday life in the south-east of the country or in the capital Kyiv. Some switch back and forth between the two languages, using Russian in everyday family life and Ukrainian at school or work; others consistently speak one of the two, regardless of whether their counterpart speaks Ukrainian or Russian. Others again make a conscious decision to speak more Ukrainian in their everyday lives. There are signs that the ongoing war is reinforcing this effect, although in the current situation it is also very clear that identification with the Ukrainian state and resistance to the Russian invasion have nothing to do with the language spoken by a Ukrainian citizen.

What is happening here before our eyes is not the sudden 'birth of the Ukrainian nation', as Western media and public discourse tend to claim, but the continuation of a trend that has been well documented empirically for many years and has intensified since the beginning of Russia's war against Ukraine in 2014. The importance of an inclusive identity tied to the Ukrainian state in its 1991 territorial boundaries has grown steadily and has been the dominant identity category in sociological surveys conducted by various polling institutions for several years. Its exact distinction from other identities remains blurred, but the trend is undisputed. It expresses a belonging to a state characterized by diversity, which in its political development has increasingly seen its population distinguish itself and its political path from Russia.

3

Protest and Transformation

The story of a transformation can be told in different ways. Often, institutions, elites and electoral dynamics are placed in the foreground. In Ukraine, the close connection between protest and transformation offers an alternative starting point that turns society into the main actor. Ukraine's transformation since 1991 has been marked by multiple cycles of mass protests. Moments of mass mobilization are generally rare in history; a concentration of such moments is all the more significant. Mass protests are associated with hopes and disappointments, personal experiences of political participation, and activist networks that often outlast the moment itself. Mass mobilization makes a further wave of protest more likely, especially if the government does not systematically suppress political opposition. However, the increased odds are not the same as an accurate prediction of future protests, and even an increase in the likelihood says little about the exact moment when discontent will be unleashed in the form of broad-based social mobilization. Even a severe economic crisis does not automatically lead to mass protest – a further trigger will be needed to mobilize parts of society. Sometimes the actual trigger seems arbitrary, since there have been many similar moments before that could have unleashed a similar force. Often the trigger is linked to a political mistake made by the incumbent government, due to it misjudging the societal response. Mass protests are nowadays predominantly an urban phenomenon. Their demands for change usually focus on a change of power at the top of the political system, although in the longer run this often does not suffice to guarantee the implementation of consistent reforms. Beyond their immediate political effect, moments of mass mobilization leave their mark on society, for example on the level of interest in politics, the range of expectations, the forms and intensity of political and social engagement, and the personal and organizational networks that outlive the initial protest.

In the Gorbachev era, Ukraine was one of the Soviet republics in which people took to the streets to demand reforms and independence. The Chernobyl reactor disaster in 1986, and the Soviet leadership's attempt to cover up the extent of the accident, unleashed a willingness to protest and strengthened the independence movement. In January 1990, people formed a human chain from Lviv to Kyiv. This was a continuation of the 'Baltic Way', a human chain that had connected Estonia, Latvia and Lithuania in August 1989 in a powerful expression of the quest for independence. The 'Revolution on Granite' in August 1990, supported by the Ukrainian student movement, was the first major protest on the central square in Kyiv. Parallel to the student protests and hunger strikes, tens of thousands of people took part in solidarity marches and national strike movements. The square, which at the time was named after the October Revolution, is now known as Independence Square (Maidan Nezalezhnosti). It shaped the aesthetics of a protest culture that was continued in later protests.

After two weeks, the Acting Chairman of the Council of Ministers of the Ukrainian SSR, Vitalii Masol, resigned. The protesters also demanded new parliamentary elections, a guarantee that Ukrainians would only have to do their military service outside the Ukrainian SSR with their consent, the establishment of a commission for the nationalization of property held within the Ukrainian SSR by the Communist Party of the USSR and the youth organization Komsomol, and the refusal to sign the new Union Treaty in summer 1991 (with which Gorbachev had hoped to rescue the Soviet Union by transforming it into a confederation without the Baltic states).

The last government of the Ukrainian SSR prepared the population for independence and endowed it with bottom-up legitimacy. The referendum on independence, held on 1 December 1991, had a mobilizing effect, and the clear majority vote in favour created a common point of reference for the period thereafter. Between 1991 and 2013, Ukraine's political system oscillated between an unconsolidated democracy and forms of semi-authoritarianism. The powers of the executive and the legislature remained disputed, with the 1996 constitution eventually enshrining a compromise which, in its deliberate ambiguity, only caused further institutional conflicts. The president's decree powers, the imprecise division of responsibilities between the president and the government, and the weakness of parliament vis-à-vis the executive were all obstacles to Ukraine's transformation into a democratic market economy and enabled oligarchic interests to exert far-reaching political influence. The country's energy dependence on Russia, for example, became a lucrative business for the Ukrainian economic elites.

Under President Leonid Kuchma (1994–2004), the political system came to resemble the model of 'competitive authoritarianism', as defined by political scientists Steven Levitsky and Lucan Way. The concept draws attention to the fact that authoritarian systems can also learn from democracies and copy elements from them which they then use flexibly for self-preservation purposes. A degree of electoral competition in a context of unfree and unfair elections is the hallmark of this type of system. Thus, there is no level playing field, but supposedly controllable alternative candidates are allowed to compete in elections. This results in at least a residual risk for the incumbent. In the presence of excessive electoral manipulation, this risk can tip into mass mobilization against a falsified election outcome or against repression of protest in the aftermath of an election. The Orange Revolution of 2004 illustrates this trend, while Ukraine more generally demonstrates how waves of protest emerge and build on each other over time, how they are interlinked through the people who participate and the ideas they formulate, and how they shape society in the long run.

One of the largest waves of protests, which expanded networks, political coalitions, expectations and demands, was the 'Ukraine without Kuchma' protest. At the end of November 2000, Oleksandr Moroz, the leader of the Socialist Party, made public an audio recording that implicated President Kuchma in the murder of the investigative journalist Georgii Gongadze. 'Kuchmagate' became the trigger for street protests demanding the resignation of the president. A protest camp remained on the Maidan for about two weeks, but the protesters' access to the square was then blocked shortly before New Year's Eve. The second phase of the protests followed in mid-January 2001. In terms of numbers, this was the largest protest to date, with over 100,000 people mobilizing against the corrupt political system and the neglect of their socioeconomic needs. The interior minister and the head of the security services resigned, but Kuchma managed to cling on to power. However, he was unable to act on an earlier referendum that was supposed to allow him to extend his term in office. The pent-up social discontent was released at the next political opportunity, which came during the presidential elections in autumn 2004.

The rigged elections in October/November 2004, with which Kuchma aimed to install Viktor Yanukovych as his successor and secure his own personal immunity, were not tolerated by the electorate. What followed was one of the most important 'colour revolutions' in history – the Orange Revolution, named after the ubiquitous colour associated with the opposition candidate and the protests. The term 'colour revolutions' is a collective term used to describe the mass pro-democracy protests that have taken place regionally and globally since the late 1990s in Eastern Europe, the Middle East and Asia. They were connected through a flow of ideas and practices, and sometimes through members of activist networks moving between different sites.

The momentum of these protests in many cases brought about a turnover in government or new elections, but the political changes often remained limited or were even reversed. In Russia, the colour revolutions, in particular the Orange Revolution in Ukraine, were perceived as coup attempts aiming at regime change directed by the West, especially the United States. The balance between internal and external actors in these revolutions has also been controversial in Western reporting and debate. While democracy promotion has been a US foreign policy priority since the mid-1980s, the US stepped up the training and funding of pro-democracy activists in the late 1990s, most notably in the 'Bulldozer Revolution' in Serbia to remove Slobodan Milošević. However, the simple fact that democracy promotion from the outside can be a background condition over a longer period of time, while mass protests materialize suddenly and only at particular moments, points to the critical importance of internal social and political dynamics in bringing about mass mobilizations.

A comparative analysis of the colour revolutions shows that they needed the right internal or regional conditions in order to unfold. Democracy promotion – or the promotion of authoritarianism by other external actors – should therefore be understood as a kind of amplifier when the domestic political conditions are right. In Ukraine, both the opposition candidate Viktor Yushchenko and Kuchma-favourite Yanukovych received financial support from abroad in 2004, the former from the West, the latter from Russia.

The Orange Revolution was triggered by the run-off between Prime Minister Yanukovych, who cooperated closely with Kuchma and his interest groups from south-eastern Ukraine, and the opposition candidate Yushchenko from the party Our Ukraine (*Nasha Ukraina*). According to the official election results, after the first round Yushchenko had achieved 39.87 per cent of the vote and Yanukovych 39.32 per cent. Even this result was widely doubted. When Yanukovych emerged victorious from the run-off with an alleged three-percentage-point lead – even though independent exit polls had predicted a clear lead for Yushchenko – protests began to build quickly. The activist movement 'It's Time!' (*Pora!*) – a slogan borrowed from the Serbian opposition – cooperated closely with the party-political opposition, which united different political camps. Together they facilitated and coordinated a mass mobilization that, at its peak, gathered about 500,000 people in Kyiv in one day. To the surprise of many, the Supreme Court reacted to these protests with a ruling that the second round of elections had to be re-run. In the repeat election on 26 December 2004, Yushchenko won a clear majority. However, the united opposition that had helped pave the way for him quickly disintegrated once he took office. An increasingly dysfunctional rivalry between Yushchenko and his former ally Yulia Tymoshenko as prime minister delayed reforms, and the hopes associated with the Orange Revolution failed to be realized.

Since that time, closer relations with the EU have been a clearly formulated goal of Ukrainian foreign and domestic policy. The EU was forced to react to the pro-democracy protests and reform efforts in Ukraine by adjusting its stance on several occasions. Accordingly, within the European Neighbourhood Policy (ENP), cooperation with Ukraine was particularly emphasized after 2004. The EU only gradually developed its policy further. From 2009 onwards, the ENP was relaunched as the Eastern Partnership with the aim of intensifying relations with a total of six states (Ukraine, Moldova, Georgia, Armenia, Azerbaijan and Belarus). Work accelerated on an Association Agreement with Ukraine (as well as Moldova and Georgia), intended to deal with economic and trade relations – including a free trade zone – but also with closer cooperation in foreign policy and in the justice sector, for example. It did not entail a commitment to future EU accession, although many in Ukraine wanted to see it as a step towards full membership.

The Orange Revolution had discredited Yanukovych, the candidate actively supported by Kuchma and the Kremlin. Nevertheless, against the backdrop of the divided 'orange' government and influential economic interests, Yanukovych staged a comeback in times of political instability. In 2006, with Yushchenko's support, he was appointed prime minister. This laid the groundwork for his second run at the presidency. He narrowly won the 2010 presidential election against Yuliya Tymoshenko and repeatedly tried to settle accounts with her during his presidency, even to the point of imprisoning her and making it difficult for her to access necessary medical care. Tymoshenko was released during the Euromaidan protests, but struggled to regain her former political influence. Political parties were generally weaker and less connected to activists and 'ordinary citizens' during the Euromaidan than they had been in the Orange Revolution.

Domestically, the political system under Yanukovych leaned once again towards authoritarianism – the constitutional reforms undertaken after the Orange Revolution, which had restricted the president's role in forming a cabinet, were withdrawn on the grounds that they had not been implemented in accordance with the constitution. In his foreign policy, Yanukovych initially seemed to follow the course of his predecessor Yushchenko with regard to closer relations with the EU (but not with NATO). At the same time, he returned, rhetorically at least, to Kuchma's balancing act between Russia and the West. Despite this ambivalent approach, Yanukovych genuinely surprised the EU heads of state and government shortly before the EU summit in Lithuania in November 2013 with his announcement that he did not intend to sign the long-prepared Association Agreement. Vladimir Putin had put him under pressure to join the Customs Union with Russia, promised him significant additional financial support, and threatened him with sanctions if he signed the agreement.

In 2013, a more consistent and institutionalized integration of Ukraine with the EU was already seen as a strategic threat by the Russian government. From the Kremlin's perspective, it was associated with precisely the kind of expectations and values that could one day become a danger to the authoritarian system in Russia. The discussion about Russia's security perceptions has mostly been reduced to the issue of NATO's eastward expansion, which the Kremlin openly positioned itself against. Less obvious, but every bit as threatening, was the association of Ukraine with the EU as the embodiment of a democratic alternative to Russia based on the rule of law.

Moreover, the orientation of the Ukrainian economy towards the EU's internal market limited the prospects for Russian-Ukrainian economic relations and the attractiveness of the Customs Union or the Eurasian Economic Union, with which Russia tried to secure economic and political influence in selected neighbouring states. Yanukovych's decision to withdraw his support for the EU Association Agreement led to his undoing. It became the trigger for a new round of mass mobilizations, known abroad as the Euromaidan and in Ukraine as the 'Revolution of Dignity' – the use of the latter term pointing to the conscious framing of the protests as an expression of universal human rights.

The non-signing of the Association Agreement, which was based on the idea of an approximation to EU rules in return for limited participation in its single market, may appear to be an unusually technical trigger for mass protest. The details of the agreement were probably known only to a few, but the president's refusal to sign was seen as a breach of trust and a rejection of a transformation widely associated with expectations of better living standards, democracy and the rule of law. The protests built up against a backdrop of widespread resentment about the level of corruption associated with Yanukovych. They were concentrated in Kyiv and cities in western Ukraine such as Lviv, but smaller protests also took place in many cities in the east and south of the country, and people from these regions travelled to Kyiv to take part in the larger demonstrations. The extent to which the population across the country was dissatisfied with the government and, in particular, with Yanukovych before the onset of the mobilization has been overshadowed by the dynamics of the Euromaidan, but it marks a significant stage in the history of an increasingly engaged and mobilized Ukrainian society.

The story of the Euromaidan is often told from the perspective of its end, putting the emphasis on its violent final stage. But this ignores the fact that it was primarily a peaceful mass mobilization that lasted for months and radicalized only towards the end in reaction to the authorities' use of force against the protesters.

The Euromaidan was not a nationalist, ethnolinguistic or regional mobilization. A rapid survey conducted among its participants by the political scientist Olga Onuch, in addition to focus groups and panel surveys conducted before and after the Euromaidan, offers a detailed picture of the different phases of the protests, the participants and their attitudes. Onuch's data highlight the greater diversity of actors involved in the Euromaidan compared to the Orange Revolution, and their different expectations and demands. There was no single overarching goal comparable to the demand in 2004 for a fair repeat election. The range of actors was neither fully understood nor controlled by the Yanukovych regime, the party opposition or the activist networks. This resulted in a lack of coordination and created opportunities for the mobilization of radical forces with a higher propensity for violence.

Yanukovych repeatedly misjudged Ukrainian society – from his decision not to sign the EU Association Agreement to his attempts to clear the protesters from the Maidan using special police units. This began at the end of November but only fuelled the protests further. In mid-January 2014, Yanukovych enacted a law restricting the fundamental right to freedom of assembly, and finally sent in riot police to contain the protests, which resulted in violent clashes in which about 100 protestors died. The victims have since been revered as the 'Heavenly Hundred'. During the final phase of the Euromaidan, the number of active protesters was much lower and their profile had narrowed. This period saw the formation of the radical group Right Sector (Pravyj Sektor – named after a location on the embattled Maidan), which developed into a conglomerate of right-wing extremists and eventually into a paramilitary unit. These forces had some influence on the interim government in the immediate aftermath of the protests, but at no point did they represent the Euromaidan as a whole, or the political majority. Ultimately, they failed to transform themselves into a permanent political organization.

In the presence of the foreign ministers of Poland, Germany and France, who had acted as mediators, a compromise agreement was signed on 21 February 2014. Yanukovych, the opposition parties and an informal group meant to represent the protesters agreed to settle the crisis and pave the way for early presidential elections. It immediately became apparent, however, that this solution was not acceptable to the majority of the Maidan protesters following their radicalization in response to the police violence. On the day of the agreement, Yanukovych left Kyiv and subsequently fled to Russia. On 22 February, the Ukrainian parliament declared him deposed and scheduled new elections for 25 May. There were no suitable provisions in the constitution for this kind of removal of a sitting president. The only charge that could have been derived from the constitution was high treason, but that would have required a longer investigation initiated by parliament amidst a political crisis. Yanukovych had effectively lost power when ministries, the army, the secret service and eventually also his own party, the Party of Regions, turned against him. Immediately after his escape, protesters stormed his luxury villa, which became the symbol of his corrupt machinations and embezzlement of state funds, and was later turned into a tourist attraction.

In Russian state rhetoric, the Euromaidan marks the beginning of the allegedly 'fascist' turn of the regime in Kyiv on the back of an illegal coup. The participation of radical right-wing groups in the violent final phase of the Euromaidan is undisputed, as is the fact that political representatives of right-wing organizations held about one-fifth of the ministerial posts in the interim government following Yanukovch's departure. At the next elections, however, extreme right-wing parties (e.g. Svoboda and Right Sector) received few votes and were once again relegated to being a marginal phenomenon in Ukrainian politics.

The interim government paved the way for early presidential elections, from which Petro Poroshenko emerged as the winner. He had previously held various political posts, including chairman of the National Security and Defence Council after the Orange Revolution, and Minister of the Economy under Yanukovych. He was and remained one of the richest Ukrainian oligarchs. He began his presidency with a strong vote of confidence, but also with the difficult task of addressing the expectations tied to the Euromaidan. Important new reforms were introduced, such as the establishment of an institutional architecture for fighting corruption, including a separate Anti-Corruption Court and electronic asset declarations. However, the functions and staffing of the new structures remained inconsistent and failed to guarantee either the independence of the judiciary or an effective fight against corruption. Towards the end of his term, Poroshenko himself was accused of corruption. In Transparency International's global corruption index, Ukraine in 2018, after a slight improvement, still ranked only 120th out of 180 countries – in the East European region only Russia ranked lower (138th). Among the most important reforms of the Poroshenko era was a comprehensive decentralization programme, a key element of the transformation 'from below'. The EU Association Agreement, which had sparked the Maidan protests, was also passed, finally coming into force in January 2016.

Poroshenko's popularity quickly decreased due to the slow pace of reforms, Russia's annexation of Crimea and the war in Donbas. Without his realizing it, he no longer represented the priorities and views of the majority in Ukraine, even as his modernization of the armed forces prepared the country for the next phase in Russia's war and established the army as the most trusted institution in society (just ahead of social and civic organizations). The repeated cycles of protest and disappointment with government policies had strengthened both organized civil society and individual-level voluntary engagement.

The next wave of societal mobilization came not in the form of a protest, but with the presidential elections of 2019, in which Zelensky won a landslide victory against the incumbent Poroshenko. Backed by an absolute majority in parliament, Zelensky was able to push through reforms very quickly, including in the judicial sector. In Ukraine, his approach was soon labelled a 'turbo regime'. The reforms became possible because there was no effective political opposition. As a consequence, parliament was further weakened as a political institution. Predictably, Zelensky's high popularity ratings did not last. His reform programme was marred by contradictions, and his two main goals – fighting corruption and bringing peace in Donbas – proved unrealistic in the face of entrenched oligarchic interests and Russia's unwillingness to give up on its political leverage tied to the war. Specific legal measures directed against selected oligarchs, including Poroshenko, were politically motivated. Nevertheless, Zelensky remained more popular than his predecessor, even during the Covid-19 pandemic. By the spring of 2021, his approval ratings stood at about 30 per cent.

Repeated mass protests were an important driver of the political transformation in Ukraine and helped to anchor the idea of a civic European nation in society. The experience of social mobilization fostered other forms of organized civil society and direct social engagement. According to surveys, this was accompanied by an increase in pro-democracy views among the population – an atypical trend in Europe during the pandemic (Onuch et al., MOBILISE 2019–22).

During the night of the full-scale Russian invasion of Ukraine on 24 February 2022, President Zelensky made a remarkable speech as a citizen of Ukraine to the citizens of Russia. Even though only a few people in Russia would have heard the speech due to media censorship there, it summed up for the Ukrainian population and external audiences what the war is about, and how Ukraine has been transformed since 1991: 'It is about peace and principles, about justice', Zelensky said. 'It is about international law and the right to self-determination. The right to shape one's own future. The right of every society to security. The right of every human being to live without threats. All this is important for us. All this is important for the whole world.'

Russia

4

Authoritarianism and Neo-Imperialism

How best to describe the Russian political system? This question has gained new relevance as a result of Russia's large-scale invasion of Ukraine and a further centralization of the Russian political system. In addition to commonly used but not precisely delineated terms such as authoritarianism and dictatorship, new terms such as 'ruscism' and 'rascism' (mixing 'Russia' and 'fascism') have been coined. The urge to find words for the observed brutality of the Russian regime in Ukraine and at home is bound to continue. 'Authoritarianism' is still a suitable analytical concept though, as long as it is not understood as something static, but as a dynamically adapting political and social system.

In the Kremlin's rhetoric, the political system under Putin is referred to as a 'managed democracy'. The phrase is an oxymoron. Not only politics, but also social science analysis suffers from a classification urge. Over the years, this has resulted in more and more categorizations of different kinds of 'democracy'. Above all, these classifications have one thing in common: they overstretch the term 'democracy'. Until shortly before its war of aggression against Ukraine, Russia was often described in European public discourse using the term 'democracy', albeit with qualifiers. The frequent references in Western public discourse to Russia not being a 'flawless democracy', for example, placed it in the spectrum of democratic systems and thus downplayed its long-established authoritarianism.

Although Putin was Yeltsin's chosen successor and the path to authoritarianism was laid during the 1990s, from the very beginning his leadership differed in style and substance from that of his predecessor. The Yeltsin era, with its political reforms and economic liberalization, was to become a negative reference point for Putin, the Russian political elites and society more generally. The combination of partial economic liberalization without macroeconomic stabilization led to hyperinflation and the rise of oligarchs who enriched themselves without restraint and exerted a great influence on politics. The experience of this period discredited the principle of democracy in the eyes of a large part of the Russian population before it could even be established. The Russian constitution of 1993, pushed through under Yeltsin, was based on the idea of a presidential democracy with decree powers. While most subjects of the Russian Federation were subordinated to a highly centralized presidential system, Russia's most important and wealthy ethnic republics, such as Tatarstan and Sakha, were treated differently. Yeltsin entered into direct bilateral negotiations with many of these republics (and later with other regions and territories), creating a parallel federalism of special agreements. However, he refused to accept self-determination for Chechnya and decided on a military response to the nationalist movement there. Yeltsin's political decisions formed the basis for his successor Putin's systematic expansion of authoritarianism. From his election as president in 2000 through his first two terms in office – and even more so following his return to the presidency in 2012 after stepping aside for one term to formally comply with the constitution – Putin has increasingly consolidated his personal rule. In its brutality, Russia's second war in Chechnya (2000–9) characterized Putin's early years in power and anticipated many of the military tactics later used in the Syrian civil war and in the war against Ukraine. From an early stage in his rule, Putin restricted the independence and influence of the oligarchs, installing instead an authoritarian system built around the so-called 'power ministries', the security apparatus and the military. The regime increasingly relied on the repression of opposition and the tightening of state control of the media and civil society.

The meeting of the National Security Council on 21 February 2022, broadcast on Russian state television, showed those who belong to Putin's inner leadership circle. The Council includes government and parliamentary representatives as well as the heads of the secret services. The nervousness of those present at the meeting was clearly palpable, as Putin dressed down some of his inner circle, especially the head of the Foreign Intelligence Service, Sergei Naryshkin, who became confused over the question of whether the independence of the Donetsk and Luhansk so-called 'people's republics' should be recognized, or whether they should immediately be included in the Russian Federation. It was a very public demonstration of Putin's power. The messaging was clear: Putin alone makes the important decisions – first and foremost the decision on going to war – and everyone else depends on him. This combination of power and dependency had been prepared for a long time. Pictures of Putin at his oversized oval table in the Kremlin, receiving state guests at a distance of 6 metres or more, have become a symbol of his personalized system of power (even if the distancing may have had more to do with Putin's anxiety about Covid-19 than with a conscious staging). Putin had almost completely isolated himself during the pandemic. This fact, too, led to a further narrowing of his decision-making circle, and created more room for his own exegesis of his neo-imperial claims to power.

From the outset, the political system under Putin was characterized by a steadily growing personalization and centralization of power, both in terms of decision-making and in the control over the regions and municipalities within the *de jure* federal constitutional structure of the country. The system is based on the loyalty of an elite circle that has become much reduced over time. The Duma and the Federation Council, the two chambers of parliament, have in practice been kept weaker than the constitution had envisaged. The scope for political opposition has contracted. The pro-government party United Russia regularly wins absolute majorities in elections that are neither free nor fair. Besides the ruling party, there is only the so-called systemic opposition, a small group of parties such as the Communist Party and the far-right Liberal Democratic Party, which give a semblance of diversity. These parties sometimes play the role of a lightning rod or introduce new initiatives, but they do not exert any influence on decision-making. The economic system remains based primarily on the use of Russia's vast resource wealth, especially in fossil fuels. This wealth has allowed Russia's rulers to avoid comprehensive structural change or a diversification of the economy. Despite the liberalization of the 1990s, the Russian government has never fully relinquished state control over key sectors and enterprises. Potential social discontent is cushioned by social policies financed from the export of energy resources. Any semblance of power gained by Russia's regions and republics under Yeltsin has been dissolved by Putin's centralization. In crisis situations – such as the Covid-19 pandemic or the ongoing war – the communication of uncomfortable truths or policies is delegated to the regional level. From 2008 to 2012 there was a presidential intermezzo in Putin's rule, as he had exhausted the then constitutional two-term limit. Western hopes for a 'reset' in relations between Russia and the West – with a more open political course and a 'modernization partnership' under Putin's successor and close ally, Dmitrii Medvedev – proved to be misguided. Medvedev was a case of *plus ça change*. Putin's return to the presidency came shortly after unexpectedly large social protests against the rigged Duma elections in 2011. Characteristically, Putin responded by expanding the repressive regime. He returned to rule for two more terms under the 1993 constitution. In 2020, this was revised to reset the clock of the presidential terms and give Putin the constitutional option of two further terms in office.

Over the last ten years in particular, political and civic opposition has been oppressed in Russia through a mixture of electoral manipulation, legal and constitutional restrictions and the use of long prison sentences as a deterrent. The repression is both overt and covert. The most extreme examples are the murder of the opposition leader Boris Nemtsov in February 2015 on a public road near the Kremlin, and the poisoning of the prominent opposition figure, Alexei Navalny, in August 2020. After his return to Russia following his medical treatment in Germany, Navalny was arrested and sentenced to a lengthy prison term, while his organizational network and foundation were dismantled using tailor-made laws and courts. One legal instrument of repression is the law on 'foreign agents', passed in 2012 and tightened several times up to 2022. The accusation of being a 'foreign agent' can now affect individuals who accept money from Western countries – even if only for travel expenses in connection with an event abroad. The counterpart to the Agents Act is the 2015 Act on Undesirable Foreign Organizations, whose activities are banned in Russia. This also includes a number of European foundations and organizations with civil society contacts in Russia.

A broader context for these repressive measures is created by the constant dissemination of propaganda via the state media, especially state television, which has long fostered fears about the threat posed by the West, especially the United States and NATO, while simultaneously demobilizing society. For many years this propaganda prepared the ground for Russia's war of aggression and its acceptance by the majority of the population. Independent media have been increasingly restricted or banned. Since the Russian invasion of Ukraine in February 2022, about 200 more media outlets have been blocked, including the last major independent channels such as TV Rain (*Dozhd*) and Ekho Moskvy. Many opposition journalists have left Russia. The banned media have been forced either to close or to relocate abroad.

The concept of 'digital authoritarianism' applies to the contemporary regime in Russia. Its main elements are the interwoven surveillance mechanisms, the omnipresence of state propaganda and media control, the deliberate spread of uncertainty resulting from different representations of the same event, the far-reaching control of the internet and the declared goal of establishing a 'sovereign internet'. An important element in this state-controlled discursive space has been a selective culture of remembrance and reinterpretation of Russian and Soviet history. The Second World War plays a key role in this memorialization. At the official commemoration on Red Square on 9 May 2022, the day of the victory over Nazi Germany, the war against Ukraine was presented as a continuation of the fight against 'Nazism' which Russia now has to fight alone. The political and strategic significance of this rewriting of history and its constant presence in public discourse have been underestimated in the West. This discourse emphasizes the historical continuity of Russian patriotism, Russia's great power status and its 'traditional values' which set it apart from Western values. These ideas have been enshrined in the national school curriculum and have thus become a cornerstone in the socialization of youth.

Russia's political system has been increasingly geared towards self-preservation and the active management of possible risks. Putin's perspective on the time window in which he could still counter the West, NATO and Ukraine from a perceived position of strength also fits this logic. He is also increasingly concerned about his historical legacy, as his thinking in broad historical trajectories demonstrates. The centralization and personalization of the authoritarian system has given Putin's own neo-imperial thinking exponentially more space. The paradox of the decision to escalate the war against Ukraine in 2022 is that in the medium to long term Putin and the elites around him are endangering the political system they have established. Putin not only underestimated the cohesion, resilience and resistance of Ukrainian society, but also the degree of unity within the EU and NATO with regard to coordinated sanctions against Russia and financial and military assistance for Ukraine. It is one of the characteristics of authoritarian systems that they can appear stable for a long time and that authoritarian rulers can adapt the system to their needs, but also that a sudden moment of instability can occur, which can quickly topple the regime through a confluence of factors. The unforeseen consequences of war could lead to such a moment for Putin's system.

Domestic and foreign policies are closely intertwined and jointly serve as foundations for the legitimacy of any political system. Foreign policy can serve to boost confidence and pride in the system – as seen in Russia after its annexation of Crimea. Domestic policy, in turn, defines the space, capabilities and instruments of foreign policy. Overall, Putin's popularity ratings have remained high enough over time, even if the initial steep rise in connection with the annexation of Crimea levelled off again after 2018 amidst an unpopular pension reform. Russia's war in Donbas from 2014 to 2022 did not have such a direct impact on Russian public opinion. The high and prolonged costs of the war were questioned, which was not the case with the subsidies for Crimea after annexation. The cost-benefit ratio in relation to the current phase of the war cannot yet be assessed. It is an open question whether the Russian elites and society can continue to support, tolerate or ignore a war with such devastating losses.

In times of war, polls in authoritarian societies are even more difficult to carry out and assess than in peacetime. Since the beginning of the large-scale war of aggression, both state-affiliated institutes and the independent Russian polling agency Levada have documented high approval ratings of 80 to 90 per cent for Putin and his so-called 'special military operation'. However, there are age differences: even in the data of the state-affiliated VTSIOM institute, support among the younger population (under thirty years old) has been lower – though it is still a majority. Before the war, surveys conducted by Levada regularly showed widespread dissatisfaction with socioeconomic conditions and politics in general, and a desire for change – but without seeing or seeking a political alternative. Over the last decade there have also been numerous and at times sizeable protests at the local level in many different places across Russia. Local grievances, for example over the demolition of residential buildings, the construction of rubbish dumps or the ineffective fighting of forest fires, etc., have intermittently mobilized people from different backgrounds, many of whom describe themselves as apolitical and do not connect their local claims to criticism of the leadership in Moscow. There have been exceptions, such as the protests following the rigged local elections in Moscow in 2019 or the protests in Khabarovsk that lasted over a year. They were sparked in July 2020 by the dismissal of a popular elected governor who was not a member of the government party United Russia. These protests revealed the potential for local crises to become regime crises. In crisis situations such as the Covid-19 pandemic or the current war, Putin's repertoire includes delegating responsibility for critical issues to subordinates, such as ministers or regional governors, who can be replaced or used as scapegoats at any time.

The constitutional reform of 2020 orchestrated by Putin opened up various avenues to his remaining in power beyond the terms set by the revised 1993 constitution. A constitutional amendment reset the presidential terms of office to zero, so that Putin could stand for re-election in 2024 and 2030 and thus remain in office potentially until 2036. However, he has created several options for himself and could also trade the presidency for influence through a revitalized consultative body, the State Council. The revised constitution now also refers to the duty of safeguarding the memory of the Second World War and Russia's core 'values'. The latter are closely linked to the authority of the Russian Orthodox Church and its head, Patriarch Kirill. Shortly after the amendment was approved, the regime's repressive nature took on a new quality in the context of the September 2021 Duma elections, which were more actively controlled than any before in order to minimize opposition representation.

History and diatribes against the 'collective West' have moved centre stage in the Kremlin's rhetoric in recent years. In the process, Putin has increasingly placed himself in the ranks of the Russian Pantheon of 'great' rulers, in particular the tsars. Stalin has been rehabilitated even though official attitudes to the Stalinist era remain ambivalent. Stalin is honoured for his role as a victorious war leader, while the victims of Stalinist terror receive less and less attention. The human rights organization Memorial, which had been documenting and publicizing the Stalinist past since the late 1980s, was banned in 2021. Under Putin, the 9 May Victory Day celebrations have been elevated to the most important commemorative event, celebrating Russia's military might past and present through a public display of modern military equipment in Red Square – just as in Soviet times.

The speeches and self-penned texts of authoritarian rulers contain important clues to the self-perception of the person speaking and can thus serve as signposts. The contrast in content and style between Putin's address to the German parliament in 2001 and his later speech at the Munich Security Conference in 2007 is often used to highlight the shift in his thinking and in the Russian political system towards a more assertive Russia. Both speeches, however, marked steps along the way towards a strong, neo-imperial authoritarianism. As

Yeltsin's hand-picked successor in 1999, Putin initially lacked a popular base of support in Russian society. His popularity had soared by the time of the presidential election campaign in early 2000 because he crushed the Chechen resistance and was able to credibly present himself as a bulwark against Chechen 'terrorism'. Against this background, the restrained tone of his speech in the Bundestag in 2001, after which German Chancellor Gerhard Schröder appealed for more 'understanding' for Putin, was just as calculated as the speech in Munich six years later. German and other European audiences heard what they wanted to hear in the speech, and saw it in isolation from the ongoing war in Chechnya. In 2007, Putin's position of power at home was undisputed, and in Munich he appeared more brash and forceful, speaking of NATO enlargement and Kosovo independence as provocations and of Russia's disappointed hopes for a new security order after the end of the Cold War. However, the basic components of this argument and of the political system behind it had been laid out earlier.

On 22 June 2021, the German weekly *Die Zeit* published an essay written by Putin on the occasion of the eightieth anniversary of the invasion of the Soviet Union by the German Wehrmacht. The essay was above all an appeal to German politicians and the German people, a reminder of the Russian-German reconciliation after the Second World War, of the close economic relations between the two countries, and of the hopes that were associated with the end of the Cold War. Back then, the opportunity to shape a 'bigger Europe' had been missed, Putin lamented, going on to emphasize Russia's willingness to cooperate in a spirit of partnership. He blamed the eastward expansion of NATO for the poor state of relations between Russia and the West. For Putin, NATO enlargement presented the former states of the Warsaw Pact and the Soviet Union with 'the artificial choice' of orienting themselves towards the West or towards Russia. This, in his view, was tantamount to an 'ultimatum'. There was no room in this argument for decisions made by independent states in relation to security fears arising from a history of Russian and/or Soviet aggression. Putin claimed in his essay that the consequences of this Western policy were exemplified by what he called the 'Ukrainian tragedy of 2014'. He described the Euromaidan as an 'armed unconstitutional coup' organized by the United States and supported by Europe. In a crude distortion of the facts, he blamed Western countries for the division of Ukraine and the 'withdrawal of Crimea from the Ukrainian state'.

Russia's War Against Ukraine

5

The Annexation of Crimea in 2014

Vladimir Putin reacted to the Euromaidan by implementing a plan that, as he himself later said, had long been prepared and required only the 'right' moment for its execution. The annexation of Crimea unfolded in a succession of rapid, coordinated steps that took the Ukrainian government, the Ukrainian military on the ground, the Crimean population and even Russian society by surprise.

Russia's war against Ukraine began with the annexation of Crimea on 27 February 2014. On that day, Russian special forces without any uniform insignia appeared in Crimea, quickly taking control of strategic, military and political institutions. Russia initially denied they were Russian troops and spoke only of 'local defence units'. The Crimean regional parliament was occupied and, in a closed session, Sergei Aksyonov, representing the small Russian Unity party, was installed as the new prime minister of Crimea. At the last regional elections, in 2010, his party had won only three out of 100 seats, with the Party of Regions (eighty seats) clearly dominating the political landscape in Crimea, as it did in other southern and eastern regions of Ukraine.

On the very first day of the Crimean occupation, a regional 'referendum' on Crimean independence was scheduled for the end of May. There were protests, especially by the Crimean Tatars. On 28 February the Ukrainian National Security and Defence Council decided to refrain from a declaration of war and a military response. The so-called 'referendum' was then brought forward to 16 March. The questions asked gave no real choice and were ambiguously worded. Voting for the status quo was not one of the options on the ballot. The choice was between 'reunification with Russia' and a 'return to the Crimean constitution of 1992'. However, there had been two provisional Crimean constitutions in 1992. In the dispute between Simferopol and Kyiv, the first regional constitution of 1992 had formulated the claim to a largely independent Republic of Crimea in a loose confederation with Ukraine, only to be toned down in a second constitution a few months later.

The so-called 'referendum' does not deserve the name, as it took place in the presence of armed Russian forces. According to official Russian figures, the turnout was 83.1 per cent, and a majority of 96.3 per cent 'voted' in favour of 'reunification with Russia'. The participation of Crimean Tatars was lower than that of the rest of the population, although no exact figures are available. Interestingly, the official website of the Russian Human Rights Council, which reports to the Russian president, later briefly published different figures giving a lower level of participation and approval overall. None of these figures may reflect the real outcome. It was not a democratic referendum, although it is always referred to as such in Russia's official discourse. It is a hypothetical question how the Crimean population would have voted in a free and democratic referendum. Without Russia's military intervention no 'referendum' would have been initiated. There had been no political mobilization in Crimea for independence or integration into the Russia Federation at the beginning of 2014 or in the preceding years. The idea of a referendum to legitimize independence was something that had been first promoted in South-Eastern Europe by the Badinter Committee, set up by the then European Community (EC) in 1991 to give legal advice on the break-up of Yugoslavia and managing the ensuing secessionism. Putin was thus cynically tapping into a European idea about an expression of the will of the people giving legitimacy to secession.

Just two days after the forced vote, on 18 March 2014, Putin delivered a speech to both houses of the Russian parliament, the State Duma and the Federation Council. With great fanfare and much pomp he proclaimed the 'reunification' of Crimea and Sevastopol with their 'homeland' Russia, delivered a history lesson to the assembled Russian elite, and officially put an end to the sense of humiliation endured by Russians since 1991.

The speech had an important mobilizing function in two directions. First, it mobilized Great Russian nationalism as a legitimizing base for Putin's neo-imperialism. Second, it was directed at different external audiences: primarily the West, but also other international actors who might be impressed by Russia's resolve, such as China. Putin set out a full-blown reckoning with Western policies in Eastern Europe since the end of the Cold War. The speech gave him the opportunity to expand on his historical myth-making about the roots of the Russian state in Kyivan Rus and the cultural and civilizational unity of the peoples of Russia, Ukraine and Belarus. He derived Russia's political claim to Crimea from their allegedly continuous close historical connection. The centuries of Crimean Tatar rule since the fifteenth century were omitted in his reading of history. Putin's historical sweep connected the Russian Empire to the Soviet Union and today's Russia. The Ukrainian SSR, and the referendum on Ukraine's independence in 1991, were not mentioned.

The speech deliberately played on emotions, in particular Russia's grievances about the break-up of the USSR. According to Putin, the fact that Crimea became part of another state in 1991 left both Russia and Crimea with the feeling that they had been 'robbed', but under the circumstances there was no way to take action against this 'injustice'. He claimed that 'in the hearts and minds of the people' Crimea had remained an integral part of Russia, and that this conviction had been passed on from one generation to the next. Putin appealed directly to the Germans, who, in his view, were best placed to understand the striving for reunification in the Russian world (*russkii mir*). He also spoke about the loss of Russian territory to the Ukrainian SSR in the early Soviet period, and thus was already going beyond the specific claim to Crimea and questioning the territorial integrity of Ukraine more generally.

The Crimea speech rehearsed many of the discursive frames that would later come to characterize Putin's war rhetoric. He accused the Ukrainian government of robbing 'Russians' in Ukraine of their historical memory and mother tongue through forced assimilation. Ukraine, he claimed, had been in a 'permanent state crisis' for over twenty years. In Putin's reading, the Euromaidan protests amounted to a 'coup': 'terror, murder and pogrom(s)' by 'nationalists, neo-Nazis, Russophobes and anti-Semites' who had taken power in Ukraine. This demonization of the protests has been part of the Russian state media discourse since 2014. The fact that right-wing extremist parties fell short of the 5 per cent hurdle in the Ukrainian elections held immediately after the Euromaidan – and likewise in subsequent elections, meaning they were only represented in parliament through a few direct mandates – was systematically neither reported nor commented on. Putin also claimed, contrary to the facts, that the Crimean population had opposed the 'coup' in Kyiv and had been subjected to repression because of it. He used the familiar argument that Russia had been asked for help by the regional population.

At this point, however, Putin still distinguished between the Ukrainian government – portrayed as illegitimate and controlled by the United States – and a Ukraine that was just as threatened by the West as Russia was. At the end of his Crimea speech, he addressed the Ukrainian people directly, affirming that he respected their national feelings and territorial integrity and had no interest in other regions of Ukraine. In sum, he cleverly manipulated the resonance of Crimea in the Russian understanding of history, and used it to legitimize Russia's increasingly explicit neo-imperial claims to power.

Putin's speech led directly to the signing of the treaty on the accession of Crimea and Sevastopol to the Russian Federation as two separate entities. On 21 March, the accession was ratified in the Federation Council, and on 24 March the last units of the Ukrainian army left the peninsula. On 27 March, the UN General Assembly adopted a resolution on Ukraine's territorial integrity, calling on states not to recognize the annexation (100 voted in favour of the resolution, eleven voted against and fifty-eight abstained). A similar resolution in the UN Security Council had failed due to Russia's veto. China abstained from the vote, while all other members had voted for the resolution.

Relations between Russia and Ukraine, and Russia and the West, plummeted to a new low. The EU and the United States imposed what would be a first round of sanctions in response to Russia's violation of international law. According to experts close to the Kremlin, the unprecedented EU consensus on sanctions surprised the Russian government. In June 2014, sanctions were imposed on a number of Russian officials linked to the attack on Ukraine's territorial integrity. They were banned from entering the EU and their assets were frozen. A planned EU-Russia summit and negotiations on visa issues were suspended, and Russia was excluded from the G8 (which became the G7). However, it remained a member of the alternative G20 grouping, which also includes countries like Brazil, India and China. Subsequently, the sanctions on individuals were extended several times and the assets of an increasing number of Russian businesses and entities were frozen. In addition, sanctions were imposed on imports of goods from the annexed territory, on infrastructure and financial investments as well as tourist services in Crimea, on the export of certain goods and technologies in the fields of transport, telecommunications and energy, and on the prospecting, exploration and extraction of oil, gas and mineral resources in or near Crimea. The United States and other non-EU countries also imposed sanctions. Russia responded with its own set of sanctions against individuals and the import of goods.

Irrespective of the UN resolution and Western sanctions, the annexation of Crimea de facto expanded Russia's military and political control in the Black Sea region. Putin was also able to strengthen his own leadership: in surveys conducted by Levada, his popularity rose from around 60 per cent to over 80 per cent shortly after the annexation. Social science analysis based on comparative survey research before and after the annexation shows not only rising popularity ratings for Putin but also a stronger expression of individual-level emotions such as pride, hope and trust in the state. The data suggest that the annexation of Crimea led to a greater congruence between the patriotic feelings of the Russian population and the reality they experienced. Russian identity was fusing with aspirations for state greatness and the outward projection of Russian power. The sociopolitical consensus, shortened to the slogan 'Crimea is ours' (*Krym nash*), helped to justify the high costs incurred both by Western sanctions and by the subsidies from the Russian state budget for Crimea, which were even higher than those for Chechnya under Ramzan Kadyrov.

Even though the EU sanctions were regularly extended and Western states refused to recognize the annexation, it quickly became widely accepted that a return of Crimea to Ukraine would be impossible for the foreseeable future – at least not until the end of the Putin era. This duality was clearly formulated by US Secretary of State Mike Pompeo, who issued the so-called 'Crimea Declaration' in July 2018, promising that the US would never recognize the annexation and asserting that Russia was undermining the bedrock of international law. The statement also referenced the US Wells Declaration of 1940 in response to the Soviet annexation of the Baltic states, which similarly asserted non-recognition of the annexation, but was followed by fifty years of de facto recognition.

The war in Donbas, starting in April 2014, and, in particular, the Minsk II agreement of 2015, which was meant to bring the war to an end, came at least with the hope of changing the war dynamic through negotiations, and created additional space for a subtext in Europe and the US that did not actively question, and at times even tacitly accepted, Russia's historical claim to Crimea. A common phrasing in public and private debate opened with 'It was a breach of international law, *but . . .*', only to go on to say that Crimea 'had always been Russian'. Centuries of Crimean Tatar rule and the integration of Crimea into the Ukrainian SSR since 1954, and into independent Ukraine since 1991, were frequently overlooked.

This widespread perception, like the historical narrative about Crimea in Putin's justification of the annexation, is highly skewed. The region has been shaped by the influence of many different peoples, states and empires. Since 1991, three claims derived from the history of the region have dominated its politics: the Crimean Tatar claim, the Russian claim and the Ukrainian claim. The Ukrainian claim is the only legitimate one under international law, which, in turn, leaves sufficient room for the accommodation of the main demands of the Crimean Tatar national movement.

It is important to understand the arguments behind these different claims in order to be able to contextualize the annexation of 2014. The Crimean Tatars define themselves as an indigenous people of Crimea, a status that was enshrined in law by the Ukrainian parliament only in 2021, i.e. thirty years after independence and seven years after the annexation of Crimea by Russia. The experience and the historical memory of the deportation under Stalin in 1944 have fused the national identity of the Crimean Tatars with the territory of Crimea, even though the Crimean Khanate historically had encompassed other regions further to the north and had not primarily been defined by an ethno-territorial identity. The Crimean Khanate emerged as one of the successor states of the Mongol Empire in the mid-fifteenth century. It existed first as an independent empire and later as a protectorate of the Ottoman Empire until the conquest of Crimea by the Russian Empire in 1783.

The Crimean Tatar identity and historical memory were preserved in spite of the Russification policies of the Soviet era. At a popular level, the Crimean Tatar toponyms – names for mountain ranges and rock formations – were used by the regional population as a whole, and the legends inscribed into the Crimean landscape remained part of the cultural identity of the region. The return of the Crimean Tatars after 1991 – about 250,000 people moved to Crimea within a few years – was accompanied by large numbers of initially unofficial settlements as well as the establishment of a parallel political structure. This brought Crimean Tatar interests and historical claims onto the regional and national political agenda, in particular through a Crimean Tatar assembly (*Kurultai*) and a system of elected executive councils (*medzhlis*). There were also smaller radicalized, partly foreign-backed, political and Islamic group-ings, but they remained marginalized by the tightly controlled organizational structures set up by the Crimean Tatar politi-cal elites around the former dissident Mustafa Dzhemilev. In the constitutional stand-off between Kyiv and Simferopol, the Crimean Tatars were temporarily guaranteed a fixed number of seats in the Crimean parliament. This enabled their direct involvement in the negotiations on the status of the region. Their demands for national autonomy played a role in shaping the territorial autonomy status granted under the Ukrainian constitution. Since 1991, the Crimean Tatar population and their political representatives have firmly defined themselves as citizens of Ukraine.

Russia's neo-imperial claim to Crimea derives from two historical perspectives. Politically, the Russian narrative begins with the occupation of Crimea by the Russian Empire in 1783. The cultural link is made through the (historically undocumented) baptism of Prince Vladimir in 988 AD in Khersones in Crimea, an event that is meant to establish the importance of the peninsula as the cradle of Russian Orthodoxy. Russian historiography forges lines of continuity from the Russian Empire through the Soviet Union to the present day. Crimean history and its memorialization are closely linked to Russian military history, cast in numerous monuments to the great and often extremely costly battles of the Crimean War (1853–6) and the siege of Sevastopol in the Second World War, both of which are commemorated as heroic acts of defence. Russia's strategic interest in the Black Sea Fleet is thus also of symbolic importance.

The beauty of the landscape, the history of the multi-ethnic region between different empires, and the often orientalizing view of everyday life in Crimea play an important role in Russian-language literature and art – for example in the literary works of Aleksandr Pushkin, Lev Tolstoy and Marina Tsvetaeva, or in the landscape paintings of Ivan Aivazovsky, to name but a few. These cultural references are an integral part of the Russian perspective on the region, and they have spread throughout Europe and the world via these sources and associations. Literature as a cultural export has played a part in the dissemination and multiplication of the colonial view of the region. Literature that belongs to the national and global canon informs political claims or allows them to exist unchallenged. The presence of a majority in Crimea who define themselves as ethnically Russian, and the predominance of Russian speakers on the peninsula, have been connected to the rhetoric of *Krym nash* ('Crimea is ours') from 2014 onwards, in particular as a basis for Putin's argument that Russia has a duty to protect ethnic Russians and Russian-speaking populations.

Likewise, it is possible to trace the history of a Ukrainian Crimea, though it is not primarily defined in ethnic or linguistic terms and is less present in national historiography or international discourse. There are, however, 'quieter' kinds of physical and ideational connections throughout the entangled history of the region, alongside the Russian neo-imperial perspective and the Crimean Tatar national identity linked to their experience of deportation and return. The census of the Russian Empire in 1897 recorded the presence of a Ukrainian-speaking population in the region called Taurida. Mykhaylo Hrushevsky, one of the most influential Ukrainian intellectuals of the nineteenth century, who set himself the task of writing a national historiography, remained ambivalent as to whether Crimea was part of Ukraine's history. Both in the Russian Empire and in the Soviet Union, the Slavic share of the regional population was increased through deliberate settlement policies, in particular after the deportation of the Crimean Tatars. These forced resettlements also increased the Ukrainian share of the population in Crimea, even though Russian was the predominant language in the region.

The Ukrainian claim to Crimea was underpinned by the international recognition of Ukraine's independence in 1991 within the borders of the Ukrainian SSR, and was confirmed by Russia in additional multi- and bilateral agreements. After 1991 the 'legality' of Crimea's transfer from the RSFSR to the Ukrainian SSR in 1954 was disputed in Russian politics. In Soviet times, the border change had been little more than an administrative act; the party elites never envisaged that the USSR would collapse. But with the break-up of the Soviet Union the transfer acquired a new meaning. The image of the Soviet leader Nikita Khrushchev's 'gift' to Ukraine was a Soviet-Russian construct. It first implied a benevolent act and later an arbitrary transfer that did not conform to the legal norms. The idea of the 'gift' lives on in neo-imperial Russian historiography and public debate. The Western view on this event also remains overly focused on Khrushchev's persona. But the archival evidence suggests an important economic rationale. Khrushchev visited Crimea in 1953, saw that the region was economically lagging behind, and hoped that the administrative and economic integration of Crimea into the Ukrainian SSR would boost its development.

Soviet propaganda used the 300th anniversary of the 1654 Pereyaslav Treaty between the Cossacks and the Russian Empire to set the timing for the transfer of Crimea and justify it ideologically. It is clear from party and government documents of the time that the transfer was only integrated into the preparations for the celebration of the Pereyaslav anniversary at a very late stage. The decision to transfer Crimea was therefore taken quickly. At that time, Khrushchev's position was not yet consolidated to the extent that he could have pushed through this decision singlehandedly. However, the idea behind the transfer was not new and it had been proposed by Khrushchev earlier. There is evidence that he had suggested it to Stalin in the 1940s in his capacity as Chairman of the Communist Party of the Ukrainian SSR. According to the report of an apparatchik in Khrushchev's circle, Stalin had refused. To what extent, in 1953/4, Khrushchev was also motivated by his own power calculations is unclear. After all, the economic rationale behind the transfer could also have presented a risk for his career.

The claims made about the 'illegality' of the transfer in post-1991 Russian politics distract from the fact that this redrawing of borders was not an isolated case and that legal rules were often made to fit a particular political context. In the case of Crimea, the Soviet authorities indeed took a shortcut whereby, rather than the full Supreme Soviets of the RSFSR and the Ukrainian SSR ratifying the decision, only the respective top leaderships in the presidia were involved. The 1954 transfer paved the way for the economic and political-administrative integration of Crimea into the Ukrainian SSR. The construction of the North Crimea Canal, which ensured the water supply from the Dnipro to the region, is an example of integration through infrastructure. The canal also represents a significant asset for Russia during the current phase of its war against Ukraine, as Russia has not yet found a way to handle the region's water scarcity.

As mentioned earlier, Crimea also voted for Ukrainian independence in 1991, albeit with a narrower majority than in other regions. Close relations existed between Ukrainian and Crimean Tatar dissidents during the Soviet era. Against this background of common historical reference points, and in view of the fact that the return of the Crimean Tatar population took place within an independent Ukraine, the connections between key figures in the dissident and national movements continued beyond 1991. The unregulated settlement of over 250,000 Crimean Tatars within a short period of time presented the region with major political and administrative challenges, but ultimately strengthened the connection between Crimea and Kyiv. The Crimean Tatars and their political leaders clearly positioned themselves on the side of the Ukrainian state and against the Russian nationalist and separatist mobilization in Crimea in the 1990s. The successive political integration of Crimea into the Ukrainian state took place, on the one hand, through the prolonged process of constitution-making at the national and regional levels, and on the other hand through elections. The Crimean electorate did not participate in Ukrainian parliamentary and presidential elections in lower numbers than that of other regions, and its voting behaviour blended into the political landscape of south-eastern Ukraine. Being part of Ukraine had become a lived normality for both the elites and the population of Crimea in the aftermath of the disintegration of the Russian nationalist movement in the early to mid-1990s.

The rapid integration of Crimea into the Russian Federation in spring 2014 rendered the local population dependent on the Russian state from one day to the next. Salaries, pensions and social assistance were paid by the Russia state in rubles. Russia automatically declared all inhabitants of Crimea to be Russian citizens. Living conditions deteriorated in comparison both to the rest of Ukraine and to Russia: the Crimean population paid a considerable price for the annexation through high inflation. Many private businesses had to close down. Crimea had been dependent on other regions of Ukraine for its water, electricity and food supplies. Russia invested in new power cables and a bridge connecting Crimea to the Russian mainland, but these took time to complete. The bridge alone took four years to construct. Opened by Putin himself in May 2018, it was a prestige project that physically drew Crimea closer to Russia. A replacement for the major water supply from the North Crimean Canal, blocked by Ukraine after the annexation and the onset of the war in Donbas, has not so far been found, resulting in an expansion of the arid steppe areas. The mood in Crimea since early 2014 can only be glimpsed from the reports of its inhabitants and the small number of journalists gaining access, and from a number of surveys. While the Crimean Tatar population leads a kind of parallel existence, those who initially welcomed Russia's intervention have come to accept the new reality with a sense of pragmatism. Opinion polls in Crimea conducted by international institutions and Levada need to be treated carefully due to the politically charged and repressive environment, but they have documented socioeconomic difficulties in everyday life, disrupted ties with friends and relatives in other parts of Ukraine, and a desire for easier movement across the de facto border with the Kherson region to the north of Crimea. In a context of authoritarian control, the surveys cannot reliably capture the extent of support for annexation and identification with Russia, though they do reveal the persistence of Crimean Tatar opposition.

Following the annexation, travelling to Crimea from the other regions of Ukraine was only possible via the land route, and proved difficult even for those with family connections in the peninsula. Anyone who travelled to Crimea via Russia became persona non grata for the Ukrainian authorities, with no further access to Ukraine. Within a very short time, the personal ties of many in Crimea to other parts of Ukraine were cut. Russia established its control regime by repression, especially against the Crimean Tatar population, the group that was potentially a risk factor for the new political elite in Crimea. Crimean Tatar political organizations and media were dissolved, though many relocated to Kyiv and other parts of Ukraine. A new exodus began: tens of thousands left the region, including at least 40,000 Crimean Tatars who settled in Kyiv and Lviv, among other places. For some of the Crimean Tatar population, this was their second or third displacement. In keeping with previous imperial policies, Russia pursued an active settlement policy intended to change the demographic balance in the region. Russians from other parts of the country, allegedly including Russian-speakers from the occupied parts of Donbas, were resettled in Crimea. Exact figures are not known, but estimates on the Ukrainian side speak of over 100,000 resettled Russians and Russian-speakers. Over time, a pragmatic acceptance of the annexation seeped into Western political discourse. In Russia itself, its effect on Putin's popularity and the political system gradually subsided, but as an act that had supposedly restored historical justice the annexation remained unquestioned, despite the long-term financial costs involved. The constitutional reform of 2020 tried to close the Crimea issue once and for all by making it unconstitutional to call into question the territorial integrity of the Russian Federation.

6

The War in Donbas since 2014

The war in Donbas, which began in the spring of 2014 and culminated in Russia's full-scale invasion in February 2022, represents the second phase in Russia's war against Ukraine. Russia's annexation of Crimea is closely related to the war in Donbas. Indeed, without that annexation, the war in Donbas would not have occurred in the form and at the time that it did. The annexation and its justification by Putin in terms of history and the preservation of the Russian language, culture and values sent a signal to separatist-minded forces in eastern Ukraine that any mobilization on their part would have a good chance of being supported by Russia. Without this external support, their capacity for mobilization would have been limited or even impossible from the start.

The Donbas region today refers to the two administrative regions of Donetsk and Luhansk in south-eastern Ukraine. Before 2014, the population there made up about 15 per cent of the total population of Ukraine. Historically, the broader 'Donets Basin' region also included parts of the Dnipropetrovsk region and the Rostov region in Russia. From the late nineteenth century onwards it had been an important site of industrialization, urbanization and the settlement of ethnic Russian or Russian-speaking workers. Migration from Russia continued in the Soviet period, as the region's coal, steel and manufacturing industries made it one of the most important industrial locations. After 1991 it played this role for independent Ukraine as well, even though its technologies and infrastructure were becoming increasingly dated.

The war did not directly involve the whole Donbas region, but it was de facto divided from April 2014. The so-called 'Donetsk and Luhansk People's Republics' were declared in the areas the Ukrainian government lost control over in spring 2014. The beginnings of the war in Donbas lie in the aftermath of the Euromaidan and the annexation of Crimea. Smaller Euromaidan protests had also taken place in the south and east of the country. Clashes occurred with regional forces that did not necessarily support Yanukovych, but mobilized around a diffuse mix of separatist ideas and local concerns of the population. This confrontation came to a violent climax in Odesa in early May, when forty-eight separatist protestors who had sought refuge in the local trade union building were killed in a fire that has still not been fully investigated, and over 200 people were injured in riots. The Council of Europe and the UN have repeatedly criticized Ukraine for its incomplete investigation of these events.

Ultimately, separatist forces failed to take control in Odesa, Kharkiv and other cities in eastern and southern Ukraine, but they were more successful in parts of Donbas. Similar to the situation in Crimea, there were no influential and organized separatist movements in Donbas prior to the annexation. It was by no means apparent that a sizeable segment of the population would support a separatist agenda. After the annexation of Crimea, a number of marginal, pro-Russian activist groups seized their opportunity, occupied government buildings and, in April 2014, adopted a declaration on the 'independence' of the so-called 'people's republics' of Donetsk and Luhansk. On 11 May, fake referendums were held in which allegedly more than 90 per cent of those polled voted in favour of the independent 'people's republics'. Towards the end of the year, 'presidential' and 'parliamentary' elections were also held, giving the two territories a semblance of state institutions.

It is clear from different opinion polls that only a minority of people across Ukraine were open to separatist ideas. The Kyiv International Institute of Sociology (KIIS) found in its April–May 2014 survey (without Crimea) that under 7 per cent of people viewed separatist ideas positively and could envisage either independence for their region or integration into another state. Additionally, less than 7 per cent were in favour of more autonomy in Ukraine. Donetsk and Luhansk were the only regions in this survey where just under a third came out in favour of the two separatist options (independence or integration with another state) and another 23.5 per cent supported more autonomy (KIIS 2014a). In the other eastern and southern regions, the two variants of separatism met with the approval of only 5 to 7 per cent, while a further 7 to 9.5 per cent supported an unspecified type of autonomy. These polls show stronger societal backing for separatism in Donbas than in other parts of the country, but even here it was not a majority consensus in 2014. In a KIIS poll from April the same year, about a third of respondents in Donetsk and Luhansk voiced their support for secession from Ukraine, but only between a fifth (Donetsk) and a quarter (Luhansk) supported the takeover by force of local administrative institutions (KIIS 2014b). The abstract idea of separatism was thus of greater appeal than the violent way in which this idea came to be implemented. Moreover, a certain latent approval in surveys is not the same as the successful activation of the sentiment.

Why did mobilization succeed in parts of Donbas while it failed to take root in other eastern or southern regions? This variation needs to be explained, since the background factors – such as the presence of an ethnically Russian segment (in early 2014 about 30 per cent of the Donbas population described themselves as ethnically Russian and about 11 per cent as both Russian and Ukrainian) and wide usage of the Russian language in everyday life – were found throughout the south-east, especially in urban areas.

Whether Russia would have supported separatist aspirations throughout south-eastern Ukraine at that time remains a matter of speculation. In Donbas, at any rate, the conditions for Russia's intervention were more favourable, and this potential for external support reinforced the local dynamics around mobilization. The combination of survey data and an analysis of local media discourses reveals several trends. There was no single issue or motivation that created openings for separatist ideas or active mobilization. There was higher support for separatist ideas among those who described themselves as 'ethnic Russian' than among those who described their ethnic identity as 'Ukrainian' or 'Ukrainian and Russian', but ethnicity and language were only seen as relevant issues for a minority. The separatist sentiment that distinguished Donbas from other regions in the south-east was thus not primarily driven by ethnic or linguistic criteria.

Other issues played a much more important role in Donbas in 2014, including the general feeling of having been politically and economically neglected by Kyiv for years and of being on a downward spiral, even though the region had traditionally contributed significantly to the economy, and concerns about the consequences of closer relations with the EU. The regional implications of partial or full EU integration still seemed difficult to assess for the population. When asked about their main concerns, a clear majority named economic issues, especially the fear of a collapse of the Ukrainian economy, delays in salary and pension payments and job losses. Compared to other regions, these concerns were more closely associated with a reorientation away from economic relations with Russia.

The success of the separatist mobilization in parts of the Donbas region, including the larger cities, was also due to the support it received from local security forces and regional oligarchs. Russia's active intervention involved its military intelligence service (the GRU) and intensive media propaganda against the new government in Kyiv, which was branded as 'Nazi' and 'fascist'. This propaganda reached the Donbas population directly through Russian media, but local media also functioned as an echo chamber. The regional oligarchs, for their part, remained ambivalent – their main interest was to secure their influence and wealth. They therefore showed themselves to be pragmatic and open to different political directions, using separatist sentiments as a tool to put pressure on Kyiv, for example.

The interim government that emerged from the Euromaidan responded to the proclamation of the 'people's republics' by deploying Ukrainian armed forces in a so-called 'Anti-Terrorist Operation' (ATO). Although some areas were recaptured, it proved impossible to restore full Ukrainian control over these territories. In June 2014, following the decision of the Permanent Council of the Organization for Security and Co-operation in Europe (OSCE), which included Russia, an OSCE Special Monitoring Mission (SMM) was deployed. This was an unarmed, civilian mission tasked with documenting political developments and human rights violations. In addition, a Trilateral Contact Group made up of representatives from Ukraine, Russia and the OSCE began talks in Minsk aimed at facilitating a diplomatic resolution of the war. The Russia-backed separatist leaders were intermittently involved in the talks. The label 'separatists' did not do the actual dynamics justice, however, given Russia's overarching influence. Russia continued to insist on not being treated as a party to the war and defined its role as that of an independent observer. In January 2023, the European Court of Human Rights (ECHR) established that, as of 11 May 2014, the so-called 'separatist areas' were 'under the jurisdiction of the Russian Federation' and that Moscow 'had a significant influence', providing weapons and lending political and economic support.

On 17 July 2014, the Malaysian passenger plane MH17 was shot down over the disputed area on its way from Amsterdam to Kuala Lumpur; all 298 passengers were killed. A series of investigations established the sequence of events and that a Russian-made Buk anti-aircraft missile had brought down the plane. In mid-2015 Russia vetoed a UN special tribunal in the Security Council in connection with this incident. A Dutch Criminal Court finally ruled in November 2022 against four individuals based in Russia and tried them in their absence. A second case has been pending in the ECHR since 2020, and a further case was opened at the International Civil Aviation Organization in 2022.

Without Russian military support, the 'separatists' could not have held out in the summer of 2014. Instead, the war became more costly for Ukraine. On 5 September, with the help of Franco-German mediation, the Trilateral Contact Group drew up a first ceasefire agreement – the Minsk Protocol. The OSCE Monitoring Mission now became the main institution systematically documenting ceasefire violations. However, it was unable to prevent further escalation. Putin and Poroshenko, German Chancellor Angela Merkel, French President François Hollande, and the leaders of the 'Donetsk People's Republic' and the 'Luhansk People's Republic', Aleksandr Zakharchenko and Igor Plotnitsky, negotiated a follow-up agreement in Minsk on 12 February 2015, a plan (Minsk II) based on thirteen points, which was supposed to enable the implementation of the Minsk Protocol. Since Russia would not accept that it was a party to the war, it refused to be bound by the Minsk agreements from the outset, even though one point stipulated 'the withdrawal of all foreign armed formations and military equipment'. The prioritization of the individual points of the Minsk II agreement were disputed by Ukraine and Russia from the beginning. Not even the first point, a lasting ceasefire, was implemented. Negotiated and signed under intense military pressure, the agreement as a whole was not favourable to Ukraine. Among the points of contention – in addition to the final status and electoral modalities for the territories not controlled by Kyiv – was the sequencing of the political and security-related points. Russia insisted that Ukraine should only regain control over its entire territory after all the other provisions had been implemented, while Ukraine aimed to regain sovereignty over its eastern state border earlier in the process of implementation.

From today's perspective, the Minsk agreements appear to some as having been doomed to fail from the outset, to have disadvantaged Ukraine, and even to have been a mistake on the part of the German and French mediators. But it is important to keep in mind that the agreements were born out of necessity. Minsk II prevented a further escalation of the war at a critical moment, when a more decisive Russian victory seemed likely. Without the agreements, the looming costs for Ukraine would have been even higher and its statehood would have been compromised even more as early as 2014. At that time, there was no political will within NATO to support Ukraine militarily against Russia, and the Ukrainian armed forces were not yet as well positioned as they were by 2022. In the years that followed, Minsk II provided the only framework for direct talks between Ukraine and Russia, with Germany and France as mediators. Temporary ceasefires, prisoner exchanges and humanitarian measures were among the partial successes that were not insignificant for the local population. Other points, such as local elections in accordance with Ukrainian legislation in the non-government-controlled areas, followed by a special status for these territories, never reached the implementation stage. Most importantly, the Minsk agreements provided Kyiv with breathing space, and bought time for Ukraine to rebuild its armed forces and forge an international coalition of support against Russia.

In total, this second phase in Russia's war against Ukraine had cost about 14,000 lives by the end of 2021; an estimated 1.5 million people became internally displaced persons (IDPs) within Ukraine and about another million fled to Russia. Whereas Crimea is of great symbolic significance to the Russian elites and society, the war in Donbas was primarily an instrument for Moscow to weaken the Ukrainian state in the longer run, to retain its influence over Ukrainian politics and to hold on to the possibility of limiting or expanding the war as it saw fit.

Thus, in 2014 Ukraine de facto lost control over a further section of its state border. A new border regime emerged in the everyday life of the regional population at the ceasefire line negotiated in Minsk. The so-called 'contact line', which shifted several times, shaped behaviour, views and identities. A ceasefire line initially marks a temporary border, but often it does not remain a temporary phenomenon. Its everyday reality contributes to its consolidation, as formerly integrated economic and social spaces and networks are forced to adapt. Moreover, the territorial demarcation is reinforced by the behaviour of the parties to the war. In the case of Donbas, Russia prioritized the issuing of Russian passports, especially before the Russian Duma elections, restricted the Ukrainian information space through Russian media and mobile phone networks, and initiated a (re)socialization of the population through the local education system. The blockade imposed by Kyiv could not stop these processes, but in practice it reinforced the separation of the two parts of the Donbas.

Crossing the 'contact line' was only possible in a few places. The difficulties associated with trying to do so varied depended on the distance from and access to a checkpoint, the infrastructure in place, and the attitudes and routines of the checkpoint guards. Encounters across the 'contact line' were unevenly distributed: those crossing from the non-government-controlled areas were mainly elderly people going to collect their pension payments on the Kyiv-controlled side. Crossings in the other direction were much rarer. Survey data and ethnographic field-work from 2019 show that those who came from the so-called 'people's republics' to the Kyiv-controlled Donbas had retained a sense of belonging to the Ukrainian state. At the time, half of the respondents in the non-government-controlled areas crossed the 'contact line' with varying regularity: about 14 per cent reported crossing it once a month and about 16 per cent once in six months (ZOiS 2019). By contrast, just over 90 per cent of the respondents in the Kyiv-controlled Donbas in 2019 said they never crossed the line. About 50 per cent of respondents in the 'people's republics' stated they had relatives or friends on the Kyiv-controlled side; in the other direction only 31 per cent of the respondents reported having personal contacts. In both parts of the Donbas, personal connections across the 'contact line' were decreasing over the years.

Conducting sociological research in war zones is always difficult. In the Russia-controlled part of Donbas, these dif-ficulties increased over time, not least because there was no clear baseline against which the representativeness of the polls could be measured. For independent Ukrainian, Russian and international polling agencies, the legal, ethical and technical means of access for both face-to-face interviews and telephone surveys have changed several times, leaving gaps when attempting to compare data for a particular point in time or between years. Nevertheless, even under these difficult condi-tions, it remains a task of academic research to collect and analyse the voices of those who are directly affected by the war. In the end, it is less about precisely determined numbers than about the trends that emerge from a series of surveys by rec-ognized research institutes or agencies. Over the period from 2016 to 2022, a gradual reorientation of the local population in the Russia-controlled 'people's republics' can be observed in these data. This has to do with the Russian 'passportiza-tion' policy, the increasingly controlled information space, and the pragmatic needs of everyday life. A clear constant over several years and across different polling agencies has been the low level of support among the local population for the independence of the so-called 'people's republics'. It is also clear that a two-thirds majority in the Kyiv-controlled areas of Donbas saw themselves as belonging to the Ukrainian state. Here, compared to survey data collected before the war began, identification with the Ukrainian state has grown stronger. A gradual polarization between the two parts of the Donbas has taken place with regard to state orientation and citizenship. One trend shared across the 'contact line', however, was that a majority of respondents in both parts of the Donbas regarded the question about belonging to Ukraine or Russia as being less important than the question about their personal standard of living.

Opinion polls in Ukraine generally illustrate that during the war a civic identity linked to the Ukrainian state was strengthened in comparison to ethnically defined identities. Representative survey data collected by the Centre for East European and International Studies (ZOiS) through the regular all-Ukrainian KIIS survey (excluding the 'people's republics' and Crimea) showed that between 2017 and 2018 a civic Ukrainian identity was cited by just under 50 per cent of respondents as their most important identity from a long list of options. Subsequently, the share of those subscribing to a state-centred identity varied, but it remained the most important identity category (between 30 and 40 per cent) in different formulations and contexts across years and surveys. Russia's war against Ukraine had thus strengthened an overarching state identity in its first two phases, rather than having an internally polarizing effect. Putin's aim of splitting the Ukrainian people had clearly failed.

By the end of 2013, the maritime border between Ukraine and Russia had still not been officially demarcated. At the end of 2003, both countries had signed a bilateral treaty on their joint use of the Sea of Azov and the Kerch Strait. The 1982 International Convention on the Law of the Sea allows free passage through these waters for any vessel of any nationality. Since the annexation of Crimea, Russia has considered the waters near Crimea part of its own sovereign territory. It controls both sides of the Kerch Strait, the only access to the Ukrainian ports of Mariupol and Berdyansk. It also increased the presence of its navy in the Black Sea and the Sea of Azov. The bridge connecting Crimea to the Russian mainland, opened in 2018, has hindered the access of international ships to Ukrainian ports. Only ships of a certain height can pass the bridge. Administrative obstructions and arbitrariness on the part of the Russian coastal guards, who are subordinate to the Russian secret service FSB, led to delays in inspections and searches of maritime traffic and jeopardized the attractiveness of Ukrainian ports in international trade before February 2022. In November 2018, there was a military escalation in the Kerch Strait between the Black Sea and the Sea of Azov. Two Ukrainian navy vessels and a tugboat were forcibly stopped by a Russian vessel from passing towards Mariupol. The Russian coast guard rammed the tugboat, and fired at and boarded the Ukrainian vessels. Several Ukrainian soldiers were wounded and twenty-three were arrested. They were only released in 2019 as part of a prisoner exchange, although the International Tribunal for the Law of the Sea had previously demanded their release. This direct military confrontation highlighted the continuous potential for escalation. The Ukrainian government responded to the incident by imposing martial law, initially for thirty days. It was extended thereafter, giving President Poroshenko additional executive powers. This moment thus also prepared Ukrainian society and politics for the practice of martial law, which was reactivated in February 2022.

In the second phase of its war against Ukraine, following its annexation of Crimea, Russia brought another part of Ukrainian state territory under its de facto control. This long phase from 2014–2022, which never allowed for a permanent ceasefire, led to a modernization drive in the Ukrainian army, but also brought certain habituation effects. The political elites and the population in other regions of the country did not want to become embroiled in an ongoing war. The Minsk agreements had prevented an escalation at a key moment, but they could not guarantee the implementation of any of the stipulated points. Incrementally, the EU issued further sanctions against Russia from May 2014 onwards – first against individuals and entities, then against economic cooperation in several sectors. By the end of 2021, the number of those facing travel bans and asset freezes rose to 185 individuals and forty-eight entities. The EU managed to regularly renew these sanctions every six months to a year, but since generating a consensus on this proved hard enough, further steps or a significant widening of the sanctions regime would not be considered until February 2022. From today's perspective, the EU's sanctions against Russia between March 2014 and January 2022 seem limited, but they were nevertheless a novelty for the EU. At no point, however, did they call into question the priorities of individual member states, especially with regard to the German-led Nord Stream 2 project. The dependence of individual EU member states on Russian gas and oil exports stood in direct contradiction to the sanctions logic. The EU as a whole, its member states, the US and NATO were not ready to substantially increase their support for Ukraine in 2014 or in subsequent years. The hope was to 'freeze' the war in Donbas or at least keep it at a manageable level. The fact that the annexation of Crimea and the war in Donbas amounted to domestic and foreign policy tests that only made a third phase in Russia's war against Ukraine more likely was not anticipated in the West at the time.

7

The War of Aggression since 24 February 2022

Russia's preparations for the third phase in its war against Ukraine began in spring 2021 with a large-scale build up of troops near the Russian-Ukrainian border. In a short period of time, over 100,000 troops and equipment were moved to Russia's western border. US President Joe Biden responded with an offer of negotiations, in addition to numerous appeals and warnings. In April 2021, Biden met with Vladimir Putin in Geneva. This meeting corresponded to Putin's long-held desire to negotiate with the American president on an equal footing, visible to the whole world, and thereby highlight Russia's international role. There was hope that Biden could formulate American and Western interests as part a new and overdue security dialogue, but also explore negotiable issues and thus reduce Russia's military pressure on Ukraine. The US president signalled that despite its strategic focus on China, the US also wanted to continue to actively cultivate good relations with Russia.

Western hopes fizzled out, however, before they could take further shape. In December 2021, Putin presented the United States and NATO each with a catalogue of demands connected to an ultimatum and an unspecified threat. Publicizing the demands contradicted diplomatic protocol and underlined that the Kremlin was not interested in negotiations. With these maximalist demands, Putin attempted to turn back the clock to before 1997 – the year of the NATO-Russia Founding Act, which had attempted to put the relationship between NATO and Russia on a new basis of trust and cooperative security by establishing consultative mechanisms and institutionalizing a presence for a Russian delegation at the NATO headquarters in Brussels. One of the central principles of this Founding Act was: 'respect for the sovereignty, independence and territorial integrity of all States and their inherent right to choose the means of ensuring their own security and the inviolability of frontiers and the right of peoples to self-determination as enshrined in the Helsinki Final Act and other OSCE documents'. This central clause has not been cited by Russia in reference to NATO enlargement for a long time, though it opened the way for the accession of the countries in Central and Eastern Europe and the Baltic states.

The NATO-Russia dialogue laid out in the Founding Act had already come to a standstill before the start of the third phase of Russia's war against Ukraine. Putin's demands at the end of 2021 included the withdrawal of any NATO presence from its eastern member states (the Founding Act had ruled out a permanent presence and led to the rotation of NATO forces in and out of the region), the cancellation of the declaration of intent – formulated at the NATO summit in Bucharest in 2008 – to include Ukraine and Georgia in NATO, and additional security guarantees. At the Bucharest summit, the Bush Administration had wanted NATO to offer both countries a concrete Membership Action Plan. Other member states, including Germany and France, had put the brakes on this plan in view of Russia's possible reactions and its influence in Donbas, Abkhazia and South Ossetia. The awkward compromise was an unequivocal statement in the final communiqué that 'Ukraine and Georgia will become members of NATO', but with no time frame specified and no clear path laid out. This formulation could be presented as a concrete security threat by Russia; at the same time, it did not give Ukraine or Georgia enough security.

Russia's demands in late 2021 were accompanied by a revived discussion about the alleged promises – made by Western governments to Mikhail Gorbachev in connection with German reunification – according to which NATO would not expand 'one inch' eastwards beyond Germany. The record is much clearer than the various loops of this discussion would suggest. There was no written and thus legally binding commitment by NATO or individual member states during the negotiations in 1990. In international relations, what is contractually agreed upon ultimately applies, even if the communication that accompanies the agreement can be interpreted differently and has a lingering effect on mutual trust. Minutes of talks, notes and memoirs of the politicians and diplomats involved in the negotiations record that Gorbachev was verbally assured that NATO had no intention of expanding into Central and Eastern Europe. Among those on record with statements to this effect are Hans-Dietrich Genscher, James Baker, Douglas Hurd, Margaret Thatcher and the current CIA chief and former US State Department official, William Burns. The timing of the negotiations on Germany's membership in NATO also plays an important role in the interpretation of them. In 1990, the dissolution of the entire Soviet Union, the end of the Warsaw Pact and the resulting security policies of independent states in Central and Eastern Europe were not foreseen by those involved. No treaty was concluded that could have covered all future eventualities. After 1991, the Central and East European states formulated their interest in NATO (and EU) membership on the basis of their sovereignty and security policies and thereby challenged these institutions to reorient themselves, which they did.

Cooperation between NATO and Ukraine began with the NATO-Ukraine Charter of July 1997. NATO assisted Ukraine in reforming its armed forces and security sector. Ukraine, in turn, participated in NATO-led military operations and in a NATO Response Force. NATO's own internal disagreement about Ukraine's membership was mirrored by a new domestic policy ambiguity under President Yanukovych. According to a law from 2010, Ukraine would seek partnership with NATO on the basis of its non-aligned status. The Euromaidan and Russia's war against Ukraine then changed the political position while also generating bottom-up support for NATO membership in regions that had been hesitant. Following Russia's annexation of Crimea, NATO increased its presence in the Black Sea as well as its maritime cooperation with Ukraine and Georgia. The focus was on building Ukraine's capacity to safeguard its own security through defence and security sector reforms, better training and new equipment. In practice, individual NATO member states, rather than NATO as a whole, took the initiative. President Poroshenko placed NATO accession high on his foreign policy agenda and prepared to anchor the declared goals of EU and NATO accession in the Ukrainian constitution. In 2019 the constitution was amended accordingly. Ukraine's new National Security Strategy, published in September 2020, was premised on the idea of a distinctive partnership with NATO leading eventually to membership. In June 2020, NATO had granted Ukraine the status of an Enhanced Opportunities Partner, partly in recognition of its contribution to NATO-led missions, including in Afghanistan and Kosovo. This was supplemented in 2021 by an Individual Partnership Action Plan, which provided for further support for Ukraine. The issue of NATO membership remained off the agenda. The United States and NATO responded to Russia's ultimatum in early 2022 by providing written answers to the demands. On 26 January, NATO made it clear that a general halt to its eastward expansion was out of the question.

However, it opened up some room for negotiation on the question of the nature and location of any NATO military presence on its eastern border. Russia described this issue as 'secondary', showing once again that it was not prepared to negotiate on substantive issues.

In mid-January 2022, Russia built up its military presence in Belarus with troops, tanks and artillery pieces, on the pretext of preparing for joint military manoeuvres. By supporting Aleksandr Lukashenko's violent suppression of mass protests in Belarus in 2020, Putin had increased the latter's dependence on Moscow and was able to advance the de facto military integration of Russia and Belarus. The joint military manoeuvres were supposed to end on 20 February, but they were extended. On 21 February, Putin gave a long speech, broadcast on state television. It was in essence a continuation from where he had left off in his Crimea speech. He argued that Ukraine had no consolidated tradition of statehood, and presented a potted history of his view of the politics of the Russian Empire. But above all he attacked Lenin's nationality policies. Lenin, he claimed, had granted elements of statehood to Ukraine after the October Revolution and transferred territories from Russia to Ukraine. Stalin and Khrushchev were also mentioned as those who, after the Second World War and in 1954 with the transfer of Crimea, had given territories to Ukraine and moulded the artificial structure of the Ukrainian state into its present form. Since 1991, Ukraine had, in Putin's words, unsuccessfully appropriated foreign, unsuitable models, which had led to a dead end via a coup d'état and 'civil war'. NATO was accused of turning Ukraine into a 'potential theatre of war'. On the question of Ukraine's accession to NATO, it was irrelevant to Putin when exactly this might take place – 'if not tomorrow, then the day after tomorrow' – but he asserted that the fundamental decision for it to happen had been made. He deliberately stoked fears of a NATO attack on Russia. He underlined Russia's alleged willingness to negotiate, but clearly stated a condition that showed no room for negotiation: a return to the status quo before NATO's eastward enlargement in 1997. Even though the United States and NATO had held out the prospect of negotiating the nature of the military presence, Putin's speech presented the Russian case as if there had been no response at all from the West.

The most extreme claim in this sprawling speech was the baseless accusation that Ukraine was committing 'genocide' in Donbas against a 'Russian' population that merely wanted to preserve its language, culture and traditions. The agreed ceasefire in the Donbas had never held, and both sides had been proven to have committed ceasefire violations by the OSCE Special Monitoring Mission on the ground. There had never been a 'genocide' of the Russian-speaking population in Donbas. Putin's chosen terminology was meant to emphasize the urgency of the situation to the Russian population at home, and set up a just cause for Russian military action, as under international law there is a duty on states to intervene to prevent genocide. The speech ended with the recognition of the declared independence of the Donetsk and Luhansk (Lugansk in Russian) 'people's republics'. In its substance, the speech amounted to a declaration of war against Ukraine.

Putin's speech on the day of the full-scale invasion on 24 February followed on seamlessly from the previous one. The words 'genocide', 'nationalists' and 'neo-Nazis' were used again, alongside invocations of Russia's compassion and its desire to end the suffering of the people in Donbas. His earlier remarks about the independence of the 'people's republics' segued into the claim that Russia had to defend itself and protect both Russian citizens and the civilian population in the people's republics. Putin described the invasion as a 'special military operation', citing the 'demilitarization' and 'denazification' of Ukraine as vague goals. The attack was thus primarily aimed at the government in Kyiv and not yet at the Ukrainian people as a whole. He also promised to spare the Ukrainian army so long as it laid down its arms.

In the early hours of 24 February, the morning after Russia's 'Army Day', Russian forces attacked Ukraine from different directions simultaneously – with missile strikes on the capital Kyiv and the city of Kharkiv in the east, as well as on cities in central and western Ukraine. Armoured columns advanced on three major fronts: against Kyiv from the north and east, against Kharkiv from the east and south, and with thrusts to the north and east from Crimea. The initial aim seemed to be the capture of Kyiv in order to bring about a change of government. In the course of this third phase of the war, the evolving aims were stated increasingly directly by Putin and his spokesman Dmitrii Peskov, by Foreign Minister Sergei Lavrov and by Dmitrii Medvedev, the Deputy Head of the Security Council: their ultimate goal was the destruction of the Ukrainian state and of the idea that there could be an independent Ukrainian nation.

The Russian military did not succeed in taking Kyiv in late February 2022. The assumption that the Russian troops would be welcomed as liberators in Ukraine proved to be a complete misconception. What started as a Russian blitzkrieg soon faltered. Over a year after the start of the full-scale invasion, despite all the Russian state propaganda, this lack of knowledge about its neighbour – a lack at the core of the decision-making in Russia – remains more surprising than the resistance and resilience of the Ukrainians. On their way to Kyiv, the Russian columns became bogged down in the spring mud, were disorganized in command and control, suffered basic supply shortages, and were destroyed by Ukrainian ambushes, often using Western-supplied anti-tank weapons. The Russian troops were ill-prepared; many apparently did not even know they were going to war. Bottlenecks of armoured columns on the feeder roads to Kyiv faced logistical problems and were an easy target for the mobile Ukrainian forces, which were well equipped for this type of engagement. In this phase, the Ukrainian army was able to make effective use of its own stocks as well as the first deliveries of Western weapons, especially Javelin and other anti-tank weapons, and hand-held anti-aircraft systems such as the US-supplied Stinger missiles. To take Kyiv itself, Russian troops would eventually have had to engage in street and house-to-house fighting, a scenario they decided to avoid.

Zelensky's decision not to seek safety outside the country or in western Ukraine after the start of the invasion sent a signal that was crucial for the mobilization of the Ukrainian army, for civil resistance, and for Western military support. The assumption that Ukraine would not be able to withstand an all-out Russian attack for long had been widespread among Western governments and intelligence agencies. But they had overestimated the Russian military – and underestimated the Ukrainians' capabilities and resolve. Western governments and institutions quickly adjusted their thinking and stepped up their political, financial and military support for Ukraine.

The difference between Putin's lengthy speeches delivered from his office desk and Zelensky's daily video messages to the Ukrainian people – as well as his team's use of social media, his virtual meetings with Western governments, parliaments, the EU and NATO, and his walkabouts to visit civilians and soldiers – could not have been starker. Zelensky quickly grew into the role of war president and effectively reinforced the rallying-around-the-flag effect. Despite the clear messages of defiance from the very beginning, it is noteworthy that the Ukrainian government quickly showed a willingness to negotiate. Russian and Ukrainian delegations began direct negotiations already in the first week of the war. The first talks were held in Belarus, near the Russian border on 28 February, and then near the Polish border in early March. Belarus was not neutral territory for Ukraine. The risky trip of a high-ranking Ukrainian delegation therefore underlined the Ukrainians' commitment to considering all options. The Russian delegation was composed of lower-ranking officials, casting doubts over the seriousness of the negotiations. The next rounds of live negotiations took place under Turkish mediation. Israel also made an attempt at mediation, while China – the country with the most potential leverage over Russia – chose not to play this role and drew even closer to Russia over the course of the first year of the full-scale invasion.

Russian Foreign Minister Sergei Lavrov and his Ukrainian counterpart Dmytro Kuleba met in person in Antalya on 10 March. At the end of March, the two delegations resumed direct talks in Istanbul. The Ukrainian delegation presented a ten-point plan for peace. With this proposal, Zelensky conceded neutrality in return for a Treaty on Security Guarantees for Ukraine in which guarantor states would have to pledge military support in case of future aggression against Ukraine. Crimea, Sevastopol and areas of Donbas were excluded from these guarantees. The status of Crimea was to be resolved through status negotiations within a time frame of fifteen years. According to the plan, the guarantor states would also commit themselves to promoting EU membership for Ukraine. A direct meeting between Zelensky and Putin was meant to settle the details of the agreement. The written proposal did not refer specifically to the situation in Donbas, but the Ukrainian position in the negotiations was that Russia should pull its forces back to behind the 'contact line', i.e. agree to a return to the status quo of 23 February 2022. The Kremlin immediately rebuffed the proposal to negotiate the status of Crimea and ruled out direct talks between the two presidents at this point, thereby once again demonstrating that there was little interest in substantive negotiations on the Russian side. Talks continued in April but, increasingly, the war context changed. There was a realization that Ukraine could withstand the invasion for longer than many had deemed possible, and the commitment of NATO and the EU to provide substantial military and financial support became apparent. The UK Prime Minister Boris Johnson must have signalled as much during his trip to Kyiv in April 2022. As the Russian military adjusted its approach by withdrawing from the outskirts of Kyiv and the north-east in order to concentrate on Donbas and cities in southern Ukraine, the evidence of Russian war crimes in Bucha, Irpin and other areas eroded the willingness of Ukraine's leadership to negotiate. The strategically and economically important port city of Mariupol only fell into Russian hands in late May 2022, after the city had been almost completely destroyed. Agreements on humanitarian corridors failed several times, and the last soldiers and civilians entrenched in the Azov steelworks surrendered under inhumane conditions.

Based on evidence collected by different organizations and individuals, courts will have to decide on the nature of the crimes committed during this war. The key question will be if, next to war crimes and so-called 'crimes against humanity', Russia's warfare against civilians could be legally classified as a genocide. Attacks on civilians and infrastructure have been widespread. Many Ukrainian cities and towns have been totally destroyed by Russian bombing and artillery attacks. Russia is still clearly intent on breaking the Ukrainian state and taking as much of its territory as possible. Putin and other members of the Russian elite, for example Dmitrii Medvedev, also openly talk about the destruction of Ukraine, its people and its culture.

Russia's advance on the southern city of Kherson succeeded, but plans to install puppet leaderships similar to those in Donetsk and Luhansk, capable of declaring sham independence or accession to the Russian Federation, could not be implemented by Russia due to a combination of local opposition and fluctuating frontlines. On 30 September 2022, Russia tried to secure its territorial gains and declared the annexation of four territories of Ukraine after another series of fake referenda: the regions of Donetsk, Luhansk, Zaporizhzhia (including the occupied nuclear power station located there) and Kherson. None of these regions is in fact fully occupied by Russian troops as the frontline keeps moving. By early 2023, Russia occupied about one fifth of Ukraine's territory.

Odesa is an important strategic target for Russia, as the city is currently the last major Ukrainian Black Sea port. Russia's failed assault to the north of Kherson means that Ukraine has retained a vital link to the Black Sea littoral. Under the mediation of Turkey, a maritime corridor was agreed under the auspices of the UN, through which Ukraine can export grain, other foodstuffs and fertilizer. This agreement of July 2022 was extended in November 2022 and, more recently, in March 2023 for at least two months. Off the coast of Odesa, Ukrainian forces managed to strike a symbolic blow by sinking the flagship of the Russian Black Sea Fleet *Moskva*. The back story even made it onto a stamp issued by the Ukrainian post office, featuring an image of a Ukrainian border guard showing the *Moskva* the middle finger from ashore. The image is based on an incident involving a border guard on the offshore Snake Island, when he was ordered to surrender by Russian forces on the first day of the full-scale invasion. The depiction of his refusal has become an iconic image of Ukrainian resistance. In early October, shortly after the annexation of four regions of Ukraine, an explosion partly destroyed the prestigious bridge linking Crimea and Russia. Who exactly was responsible for this act remains unclear, but it highlighted the fact that Crimea is not off bounds in this war.

Russia has succeeded in forging a land corridor from Crimea to Donbas via Berdyansk and Mariupol. The Dnipro Canal is currently under Russian control and could potentially enable Russia to resolve Crimea's water supply deficit. Despite these land gains, the Russian army has had to retreat, regroup and consolidate. In September 2022, a Ukrainian offensive quickly pushed the Russian troops out of large tracts of occupied territory in the northern and north-eastern parts of Ukraine up to the Russian border. A further offensive in the south near Kherson managed to force the occupiers out of territories north of the Dnipro River. On 21 September, Putin announced a partial mobilization of up to 300,000 recruits. This step, he argued, was necessary to fight 'the collective West'. In official Russian state rhetoric, descriptions of the war have shifted more and more toward a direct confrontation with the West and NATO. Despite the emphasis on the phrase 'partial mobilization', the war was now brought closer to Russian society. The mobilization increased the out-migration of young Russians. Recruitment was uneven across the country: higher in the poorer ethnic republics, but kept low in Moscow and St Petersburg in an attempt to avoid public protests. Subsequently, Russia concentrated its forces over the winter to take full control of the Luhansk and Donetsk regions. Even though cities across the country are being bombed by Russia at regular intervals, e.g. Lviv and Vynnytsya, an intense war of attrition is being fought in First World War-style trenches in Donbas, with relentless artillery barrages and costly infantry assaults. The battle over Bakhmut epitomizes this type of warfare, characterized as it is by the preponderance of artillery strikes and the cynical use by Russia of the private Wagner units, whose recruits from Russian prisons serve as cannon fodder. Over the winter, Russia made only small, incremental gains. Following further NATO weapons supplies, a Ukrainian counter-offensive was expected in late spring 2023.

After over a year of war, according to Western intelligence sources, the fatalities on both sides are in the hundreds of thousands, with more seriously wounded. The sheer scale of the war makes it the worst in Europe since the end of the Second World War. One of its most dramatic impacts has been the displacement of Ukraine's population. By May/June 2022, UNHCR estimates already put the total number of people crossing Ukraine's western borders at about 7 million – mostly women and children, as martial law does not permit men aged between eighteen and sixty to leave. In addition, there were an estimated 7 million internally displaced persons (IDPs). In a country with a population of just over 40 million, this means that about a third of the population has been on the move, including more than half of all children. In January 2023, UNHCR estimated that there were over 10 million Ukrainians displaced across Europe (this figure includes about 3 million individuals in Russia despite evidence of their deportation) and about 5 million IDPs. In absolute numbers, Poland has taken in the most displaced Ukrainians – by January 2023 more than 1.5 million individuals, followed by Germany with just under 1.1 million, the Czech Republic with around 490,000, Italy with around 170,000 and Spain with about 160,000 (UNHCR 2023). Relative to population size, Estonia, the Czech Republic, Moldova and Poland have taken in the highest share of displaced Ukrainians (4–5 per cent of their respective populations).

Displacement comes with ongoing movement, including moving back and forth between a neighbouring country and Ukraine. Overall, since February 2022, over 20,000 border crossings out of Ukraine and just under 12,000 into the country have been counted (UNHCR 2023), indicating that individuals have repeatedly moved across the state border in both directions. Many of the roughly 3 million Ukrainians deported to Russia have gone through filtration camps. The arrest warrants on war crimes charges issued by the International Criminal Court in March 2023 against Vladimir Putin and the Russian Commissioner for Children's Rights, Maria Lvova-Belova, focused on their responsibility for the illegal deportation of children to Russia.

It is becoming apparent that the war will continue, perhaps for several years. Ukraine is dependent on Western financial assistance and arms supplies – now including modern Western tanks, multiple rocket launchers and ammunition, and, in the near future, fighter jets. Some NATO member states have supplied consistently, notably the US, the UK and the Baltic states, as well as many East and Central European states; other NATO members were more reluctant or lacked what was needed in their own stocks. Germany initially belonged to this group, but committed in early 2023 to sending modern Leopard battle tanks, alongside the US, the UK and countries in Central and Eastern Europe that have German-produced tanks in their stock.

So far, NATO and the EU have been relatively united internally. NATO as a whole has taken a clear position, and many member states have made use of their right under the UN Charter to assist a state under attack against the aggressor. Individual NATO members, especially Germany, have been accused of hesitancy, for example by Poland and the Baltic countries, but overall NATO is aware of the importance of its unity in this war. It has remained consistently reticent on the issue of imposing a no-fly zone over Ukraine, which would make a direct military confrontation between NATO and Russia more likely. As Russia is a major nuclear power, NATO is trying to keep the risk of a wider escalation of the war under control, while at the same time supporting Ukraine through increasingly substantial arms deliveries. Equally, there are signs that the economic cost of this policy is weakening public support in some EU countries and in the US. In April 2023, Poland and Hungary banned the import of Ukrainian agricultural products, notably wheat, due to protests from their farming constituencies. These kinds of protests and policy responses are likely to increase as the war continues.

Government-to-government assistance between mid-January 2022 and mid-January 2023 has been estimated by the Ukraine Support Tracker of the Kiel Institute for the World Economy at 143 billion euros, of which the US accounted for just over half (about 70 billion euros), followed by the EU institutions with about 55 billion euros. When measured as a percentage of GDP, the Baltic states and Central and East European states like Poland, the Czech Republic and Bulgaria rank highest, but the US also remains in the top five. With regard to military aid, European countries have committed greater shares of their stock of heavy weapons compared to the United States. The Czech Republic topped the list, with 32 per cent of its stock committed, followed by Norway, the UK and Poland (20–25 per cent of stock committed). By comparison, the US commitment in the same time period accounted for just under 4 per cent of its heavy weapons stocks. Poland is the only country that by January 2023 had already delivered what it pledged. At the end of February 2022, the German Chancellor Olaf Scholz delivered a speech in parliament about the *Zeitenwende* ('turn of an era'), which broke with the post-Second World War consensus in Germany on not sending military aid abroad, and captured a sentiment across Western Europe and the West. In historical terms, this rethinking on the part of the German government and German society came quickly; however, actual deliveries and the training of Ukrainian soldiers appeared slow to both the Ukrainians and the Central and East European states.

In the run-up to the invasion the EU had agreed on a series of sanctions and threatened Russia with them, though without specifying their type, depth or sequencing. On 22 February 2022, the German government halted the Nord Stream 2 gas pipeline. The following day marked the start of many rounds of new EU sanctions. In addition to targeted sanctions against individuals linked to the recognition of the 'people's republics' and the invasion, sanctions applying to financial, trade, energy, transport, technology and defence sectors were rolled out step-by-step. Many of them had been unthinkable previously, but they quickly became the new norm: Russian banks were excluded from the international payment system SWIFT and additional export controls were imposed; a more restrictive visa policy and a ban on Russian broadcasters abroad were introduced. An EU coal embargo was implemented with a transition period, as well as an embargo on imports of Russian crude oil and refined petroleum products, with exemptions for Hungary and Slovakia. The US, UK, Canada, Switzerland and other countries also imposed sanctions. In an unprecedented step, Russia's sovereign foreign currency holdings held abroad were frozen. By February 2023, ten packages of EU sanctions had been introduced. Travel bans and asset freezes had been imposed on close to 1,500 individuals and over 200 entities (in April 2023 the Wagner Group was added to this list).

Nevertheless, after an initial period of uncertainty at the outset of Western sanctions, the Russian Central Bank has managed to stabilize the economic situation inside Russia by keeping the depreciation of the rouble to a minimum and inflation lower than expected. Russia has retained control of a sizeable reserve of foreign currencies and gold amounting to about 300 billion dollars, and adjusted quickly to the need to replace Western products with home-produced goods. It has also sharply increased its trade with China, India and other countries in the Global South. Russia's limited access to financial and capital markets and to Western technology will have an effect on its economy and military in the medium and longer term, but this has not yet had a direct impact on the state of the war. In the short run, Russian energy exports have been redirected to China and India, earning Russia a higher income than in the past. In 2022, it exported more oil than at any other time in the past.

Already on the day after the invasion, the UN General Assembly passed a resolution declaring Russia's attack illegal under international law and calling on Russia to immediately stop its war of aggression. Out of a total of 193 states, 141 supported the resolution. Apart from Russia, only four states voted against: Belarus, Syria, North Korea and Eritrea; thirty-two states abstained, including China and India. The UN Security Council is powerless in this matter due to the veto power of Russia and China's abstention. In April 2022 the UN General Assembly passed a resolution on the exclusion of Russia from the UN Human Rights Council. Here, the distribution of votes was already different, highlighting the varying prioritization of human rights across the UN states: ninety-three states voted in favour of the resolution, twenty-four were against and fifty-eight abstained. These votes showed that Russia is not as internationally isolated as is often claimed in the West. Many states in the Global South do not see the war as their war. Many are neutral or favourably disposed towards Russia, and many bypass the sanctions regime – including India, Brazil, Israel, Turkey and South Africa. China has intensified its strategic cooperation with Russia. A third resolution by the UN General Assembly on 23 February 2023, again calling on Russia to end the war and withdraw from Ukraine, reaffirmed the global positioning from the start of the invasion a year earlier: 141 states voted in favour, seven voted against (the Democratic Republic of Congo and Mali in addition to the previous list of countries) and thirty-two abstained, again including China and India.

8

The Consequences of the War

The war will have a lasting impact not only on Russia and Ukraine, but also on reconfiguring international relations more widely. The consequences of the war extend beyond the high number of fatalities, wounded and displaced and the enormous scale of destruction. This chapter does not present an exhaustive list, but rather outlines a range of already apparent and possible future effects. A war of this dimension also brings into focus the consequences of regional and global dependencies that, while long known, have been underestimated in terms of their political and security significance. These include energy and food dependencies, and an anti-Western sentiment in parts of Africa, Latin America and Asia. That sentiment, shaped by the legacies of colonialism, explains why elites and societies in the Global South tend to be neutral towards the war and regard current and future relations with Russia as a kind of insurance policy in case relations with the West turn sour again.

Change of perspective

One of the most obvious effects of the war is the global attention Ukraine has received since 24 February 2022. This focus opens up different perspectives, but the conclusions drawn from these and how they are translated into policy responses varies across countries and political actors. The fact that Ukraine is now to the forefront in the physical and mental map of various international institutions, governments, economic actors and populations allows for a more differentiated view of Central and Eastern Europe. This change is taking place not only at the level of the political elites, but also at the societal level. The perceived distance of Ukraine is decreasing, anchoring it in Europe. In defending its independence and statehood, the country is freeing itself from Russia's colonial slipstream and inscribing itself in the European public consciousness. In this sense, the centre of gravity in Europe along multiple dimensions is shifting eastward.

Ukraine

What the future borders of the Ukrainian state will look like is uncertain at this stage. It remains an open question whether and how far the Russian occupation can be pushed out of the south-east of the country, including Crimea, by the Ukrainian armed forces with the help of Western arms supplies. Anyone who pretends to be able to answer it underestimates the dynamics of military developments. Even the level of physical destruction and its consequences can only be grasped in rudimentary terms so far. Reconstruction, in particular if it is conceived and implemented as a transformative rebuilding of Ukraine, will take many years, if not decades, especially if the war is waged over a long period of time characterized by phases of varying intensity.

Reconstruction includes not only the repair costs but also the economic damage. According to an analysis by the Kyiv School of Economics, the repair costs already amounted to just over 100 billion euros after the first 100 days. The destruction mainly included residential buildings and roads. The International Monetary Fund and the World Bank also estimated that the Ukrainian economy would collapse by 40 to 45 per cent in 2022 – Ukrainian figures speak of a 30 per cent contraction. According to the Ukrainian government and the Kyiv School of Economics, 600 billion US dollars were already needed for reconstruction, including infrastructure, by mid-May 2022; outside Ukraine, figures of up to 1 trillion US dollars are circulating. According to Ukrainian government reports, the destroyed infrastructure at the end of May 2022 already included about 2,000 educational institutions, over 600 medical facilities, 24,000 kilometres of roads, and one third of the registered airports (eleven out of thirty-six). Since late 2022, Russia has systematically destroyed large parts of Ukraine's electricity grid. The Ukrainian Ministry of Culture has also registered about 800 crimes against Ukraine's cultural heritage. By January 2023, over 230 destroyed sites had been verified by UNESCO. Among the cultural assets affected are many churches, as well as monuments, museums, theatres and libraries. Attacks on civilian facilities and on cultural heritage count as war crimes under international law. The destruction of cultural property has been less of an international focus; nevertheless, what Putin's goal is becomes particularly clear here. Cultural assets are the historical sources and the concrete spatial and temporal reference points of memory and identity for a nation. Unlike infrastructure, which can be rebuilt, destroyed culture is less easily replaced. The war against Ukrainian culture is indicative of Putin's ultimate war aim. A central question for reconstruction will be what to rebuild as closely as possible to the original and what to deliberately build differently to adapt it to today's needs and make it more habitable, energy-efficient or participatory. Reconstruction is therefore a balancing act between restoration and transformation. The biggest challenge will be to coordinate this process in order to actively involve society and link it to the wider internal reform process. In Ukraine as well as in the EU and the United States, the Marshall Plan for post-Second World War reconstruction is increasingly used as a reference point. By way of comparison, the Marshall Plan, named after the then US Secretary of State George C. Marshall, provided about 13 billion US dollars (just over 100 billion in today's money) to more than a dozen countries between 1948 and 1952, according to the guidelines of a central authority. The largest sums went to the United Kingdom and France, with the Federal Republic of Germany in third place. The support had strategic goals going beyond direct financial aid, addressing the need for economic reconstruction, better living conditions and prosperity; it was also tied to integration into the US-led Western Alliance. We can expect something similar to happen with Ukraine, though here the EU Commission is likely to be tasked with at least parts of the coordination in order to synchronize the process with EU integration.

The war is already changing the political landscape in Ukraine. Under martial law, in force since March 2022, Zelensky banned the political forces that had long been dominant in the south-east and through which Russia exerts or could exert influence. The ban mainly affected the then largest party of the south-east, the 'Opposition Platform – For Life', whose leader, Viktor Medvedchuk, has close personal ties to Putin and was involved on the Russian side in the Ukrainian-Russian negotiations following the invasion in February 2022. The party and its predecessor – the Party of Regions of former President Viktor Yanukovych, against whom the Euromaidan protests were directed – can best be described as loose conglomerates of economic and political interests marked by internal rivalries. The regional oligarchs behind these and similar, smaller parties are not fixed on Russia in their economic orientation. Many had been consciously turning towards the West for years, benefiting more from closer economic relations with the EU than Ukraine's many small or medium-sized businesses. The term 'pro-Russian parties' has therefore always been a misnomer. What united the oligarchs was rather their aim of obstructing the anti-corruption reforms that impinged on their interests rather than cultural issues or integration with Russia.

The current ban on parties applies until the end of martial law. Even without the ban, the war has begun to undermine political loyalties and the loosely defined parties, in particular at the local level. The richest and most influential Ukrainian oligarch, Renat Akhmetov – who owned, among other things, the bitterly fought-over Azov Steel plant in Mariupol – has clearly sided with the Ukrainian state recently, despite his disputes with Zelensky. It is not impossible that oligarchic interests will reorganize themselves on the basis of parties during the war or afterwards, but they too will have to adapt to the conditions created by the war. Many of them have lost a sizeable part of their assets. The process of rebuilding Ukraine with the help of Western funds is likely to provide incentives for new and old oligarchs, but their main interests will be oriented towards the integration of Ukraine into Western structures, most notably the EU. The border between Ukraine and Russia has hardened in every respect to such an extent that it is difficult to imagine economic relations across it, including through the pipelines across Ukraine.

Internal and external displacement have generated new networks between Ukrainians from different parts of Ukraine. The shared experience of war and displacement has reduced the perceived distance between Lviv and Severodonetsk or Donetsk, which was still felt after 2014. A change in language practice is also emerging more clearly as a consequence of the war. Identification with the native language Ukrainian, a symbolic category that cannot be equated with the everyday spoken language, had continued to rise in recent years and will be further strengthened. Going beyond the more symbolic category of the native languages, there is evidence that Russian-speaking Ukrainian citizens are consciously switching to Ukrainian in their everyday lives. We can expect this to be a long-term trend.

Social structures are both destroyed and created during war. Ukraine had built an active civil society over many years, especially after 2004 and 2013–14. Due to the fact that many civil society actors quickly became involved in national defence during the early stages of the war, either in the army or in territorial defence units, prominent representatives of civil society are now also among the dead, wounded and traumatized. Internal and external displacement also deprive civil society structures of some of their resources for engagement. However, almost the entire society is mobilized currently in one way or another, thus creating the basis for a new or expanded civil society, and a wider range of social engagement beyond an institutional definition of civil society. This could either help to build a stronger and democratic state from below – or it could continue to compensate for what the state is not capable of doing. If social policy does not sufficiently target vulnerable groups in the aftermath of the war, their disappointed expectations could make for instability. As those displaced beyond the borders of Ukraine will not be able to return to Ukraine immediately – and some will not return at all, in particular if the war lasts for years – it will be a challenge to find ways to include them and their expertise in the reconstruction of the country.

The experience of war traumatizes both those fighting at the front and those left behind or displaced. A whole generation of men and increasing numbers of women are being killed, wounded or disabled, and a whole generation of all age groups is being traumatized. The experience of other war contexts demonstrates that trauma of these dimensions stays with people and even becomes a cross-generational legacy. Military commanders and veterans are likely to play a prominent role in politics. Zelensky may well be dependent on his army generals for his political future. Valerii Zalushnyi, Commander-in-Chief of the Ukrainian Armed Forces, could well emerge as a political player in his own right, possibly as a rival to Zelensky. The question of who did what during the war is likely to take on political salience in the future and could divide rather than unite society. Resentment and hatred of Russia will also leave a mark on domestic legislation, for example in educational and cultural policy, historiography and memory politics, and policies on penalizing collaboration with the Russian occupiers. Wartime politics centralizes decision-making. The concentration of power around the president, coupled with an emphasis on technocratic expertise during reconstruction, could deepen centralization within the political system. Parliament, due to its necessary reorganization on the basis of new parties and blocs, could be sidelined, and there is a risk of the pre-2022 decentralization slowing down or derailing. On the other hand, the structures and processes around decentralization, and the horizontal connections formed at the local level during the war, could provide an important corrective to centralization at the national level.

The complex situation of the churches in Ukraine is also changing as a result of the war. Since 1992, Ukrainian Orthodoxy has been internally divided between the Moscow and Kyiv Patriarchates. In early 2019, the Orthodox Church of Ukraine was recognized as independent by the Ecumenical Patriarchate of Constantinople. The war of aggression since February 2022 has also led the Ukrainian Orthodox Church of the Moscow Patriarchate to partially distance itself from Moscow. Whether this will lead to reconciliation within Ukrainian Orthodoxy, however, is uncertain, as the Ukrainian Orthodox Church of the Moscow Patriarchate is widely perceived as being directly linked to the Russian regime and its security services. Abroad, too, new tensions are arising in church circles as well as among the displaced from different backgrounds. The foreign parishes of the Orthodox Church often belong to the Moscow Patriarchate and are now confronted with the challenge of taking a position in view of a changing religious community.

Russia

The three phases of the war have had and are still having different effects on Russia itself. While the annexation of Crimea increased support for Putin and boosted a range of positive emotions vis-à-vis the Russian state, the war in Donbas did not lead to a comparable emotional mobilization, but prepared Russian elites and society for a long-lasting war. The Russian government is now building on this by redefining the war as a civilizational war, which is framed as existential for the Russian state and its people. Often the emphasis is on the Russian people, at other times the ethnic diversity of the Russian state is acknowledged. The idea of an existential threat has been a constant in the state propaganda designed to undermine the notion of an independent Ukraine and to mobilize Russians against the West.

The short- but also the medium- and long-term effects of the full-scale invasion will be more far reaching for Russia than those of the first two phases of its war against Ukraine. The first immediate effect is a further tightening of the authoritarian system: decision-making is limited to an even narrower circle around the president. From the outside, it is not apparent who Putin includes in his inner circle. Defence Minister Sergei Shoigu and Chief of General Staff Gerasimov have been pictured in talks with Putin, but these images simultaneously reflect subordination and distance. The head of the mercenary Wagner Group, Yevgenii Prigozhin, and the Chechen leader Ramzan Kadyrov, both of whom command groups of fighters at the frontline, have begun to assert themselves politically as war hawks. They publicly criticize Putin and the army for not fighting effectively, but they do not as yet challenge the Russian president. For the moment, there is little indication that Putin's position is weak, but if the war proves too costly – both in terms of lives lost and the economy – a split within the elite, possibly including regional mobilization against the centre, is among the possible scenarios. Most likely this would not entail a renewed democratization but rather an authoritarian system without Putin. Even if it is impossible to predict who will emerge as his successor(s), the system may look rather similar after his departure, or even be more militaristic. The war may not enter the history books as Putin's heroic legacy, but it will determine his fate as president.

The tightening of autocracy also includes a further expansion of repression against anyone who questions the war and, by extension, Putin's leadership. The word 'war' must not be used – in Russian official parlance it continues to be a 'special military operation', a phrase intended to imply that a necessary and carefully controlled military intervention is being carried out. Heavy prison sentences and fines can be imposed both for using the word 'war' and for any protests against the war. This put an end to the anti-war petitions and protests of the first days and weeks after 24 February. Any independent media that still existed were closed down or seized by the state. The plan to give Russia a 'sovereign internet' was also accelerated. Access to blocked content is still possible via VPN and messenger services, but this requires know-how in terms of actively searching for alternative sources of information. For Russia the war is about Ukraine but also about its confrontation with the political and cultural 'West'. Politics and the economy have been subsumed under the war effort, and in this mode Russia can continue for quite a while, probably years.

The effects of the sanctions packages gradually imposed by the EU and the United States have been cushioned by Russia's reserves of about $600 billion accumulated over recent years (although around $300 billion of that has been frozen in foreign accounts), but the active financial policy of the Russian Central Bank, a rise in commodity prices, and increased commodity exports from China and India have also relieved the pressure. Moreover, some EU countries continue to import oil (Hungary) and gas (Austria). Following the far-reaching economic sanctions against Russia in the aftermath of February 2022, Russian citizens experienced price increases on many products, bouts of hoarding and temporary caps on cash withdrawals in foreign currencies. Inflation seemed set to rise but the Central Bank's financial policy has limited this risk.

The EU's sanctions packages followed the logic of gradually increasing pressure on Russia while maintaining the necessary consensus and staying-power in the West. However, the fact that Western countries could not initially agree on comprehensive energy embargoes due to their large but uneven dependencies – and eventually decided on partial, time-delayed embargoes for coal and oil – left some leeway for trade with Russia. The immediate pressure on Russia's population will increase when the supply of spare parts to production facilities begins to dry up, and access to technology cannot be replaced easily in the short term, including from China. However, the political implications of this increasing economic pressure are unclear. Criticism of the government will not necessarily mobilize pressure from below, and an even higher dependence on state aid may also contribute to the population becoming even more apolitical or more nationalistic and pro-state.

It is estimated that hundreds of thousands of mostly younger and well-educated Russians have left the country for political reasons but also to avoid the draft. Armenia, Georgia, Kazakhstan, Kyrgyzstan and Turkey have been among the main destinations, as they are easier to access under current regulations. Emigration of this kind constitutes a brain drain, but it also rids the political system of potentially vocal opposition. In the long run, access to Russia from outside will remain virtually impossible for Western academia and civil society. This will reduce Western expertise on Russia, in particular Russian society. To get beyond a new type of Kremlinology, it can only be replaced to a certain extent by research based on externally accessible sources and Russian experts in exile. The biggest open questions are how long the reality of this war, including its casualty figures, can be kept from the Russian people, and how, when the facts become clear to them, individuals and society as a whole will position themselves vis-à-vis the regime and face up to the reality and the associated question of guilt. This process will be a task for several generations. For the time being, Russian society is either trying to keep the war at a distance or is actively supporting it.

The EU and NATO

The EU has more or less managed to maintain a consensus in its policy towards Russia since the beginning of 2022. However, it has also become apparent that in a crisis of this kind EU sovereignty is not (yet) a reality. In terms of the transatlantic partnership, it has depended once again on US leadership, which has been proactive on Ukraine under the Biden administration but could take a different approach after the next presidential elections in 2024. The EU could rise to the challenge and turn itself into a more independent foreign and security policy actor, based on its military capabilities, or it could fail to manage its internal political divisions, become more rather than less dependent on the US – in particular in its confrontation with China – and gradually become less important globally. Only weeks after the start of Russia's full-scale invasion, Ukraine submitted its application for EU membership. Moldova and Georgia followed suit shortly afterwards. In record time, on 23–24 June, the European Council, representing the governments of the EU member states, followed the EU Commission's recommendation to grant candidate status to Ukraine and Moldova. In principle, this is a historic decision – to be compared in its potential scope with the EU enlargement to the east in the early 1990s and the founding phase of the European Coal and Steel Community at the beginning of the 1950s. The key motivation at the outset of European integration was the desire to maintain peace between Germany and France in a 'solidarity of action' – in the words of the then French Foreign Minister Robert Schuman – via jointly regulated access to resources.

Candidate status is a first step on the sometimes long road to EU membership. The status itself requires unanimity in the European Council, as does the separate question of opening negotiations, which in the case of Ukraine is likely to come after the war. The decisions on candidate status, the opening of negotiations and final accession are not bureaucratic decisions reached by the EU after ticking off a list of precise criteria. The so-called Copenhagen criteria, which the EU formulated in 1993 in preparation for its eastward enlargement, describe essential characteristics that are very general and leave ample room for interpretation. The criteria refer to the stability of democratic institutions, the rule of law including human and minority rights, a functioning market economy that can integrate into the internal market, and the capacity of the candidate country to adopt the EU's complex body of rules (*acquis*). A fourth criterion concerns the EU's own capacity to absorb the new country. Beyond the political leeway in interpretation, which the EU has already used several times, these criteria are used as a yardstick both in the decision on candidate status and during the subsequent accession negotiations.

The debate among member states on the possibility of candidate status for Ukraine amidst war was controversial until the very end, and even among supporting governments much verbal acrobatics were used to emphasize the long road to full membership and the need for the EU to reform itself ahead of Ukraine's accession. With Ukraine's candidate status, however, the shared imagination within the EU is widening. This includes a sense of responsibility for reconstruction in Ukraine in terms of a gradual reform process. With this concrete perspective, politics and society in Ukraine receive a clear point of orientation for their reform process and rebuilding. The EU's track record of engagement in the Western Balkans – where it tried to combine accession with post-war state-building and democratization – is mixed. The first step towards EU membership for Ukraine is an opportunity for a revival of the enlargement logic of the EU as a whole: the meaning of the 'common values' in the EU treaties becomes tangible for everyone in times of war. Moreover, the difficult negotiations inside the EU about the different sanctions against Russia and the adoption of a credible perspective on Ukraine highlight the need for reforms within the EU itself, in particular with regard to the move from decisions by consensus to majority voting. The coming months and years will show whether the EU is up to the task or whether its internal divisions will intensify against the backdrop of the economic costs of the war felt in the member states. The Baltic states, Poland and the Czech Republic are claiming a new vocal space at the heart of EU decision-making, but the EU is unlikely to be clearly divided into east and west. The former pragmatic alliance of Poland and Hungary is at least temporarily interrupted, as Hungary is continuing to maintain closer relations to Russia.

The war has underlined the central role of NATO and the importance of strategic transatlantic cooperation in foreign and security policy. NATO as an institution is being strengthened but also changing as the war continues. Budget debates that faltered for years are now generating promises from some member states to go beyond the previously agreed but often missed target of 2 per cent of GDP spent on defence. The general trend in the EU, the UK and the US is now one of higher military expenditure. The Russian invasion caused Finland and Sweden to apply for NATO membership (with Finland acceding in April 2023 and Sweden currently trying to overcome Turkey's last reservations about its bid), thereby breaking with their long histories of neutrality. The war will only hasten the process Putin tried to pre-empt: in addition to new member states, NATO's forward military presence on its eastern border will be strengthened, and most likely will become permanent in the Baltic states, Poland and Romania, among others. The NATO summit in Madrid at the end of June 2022 signalled a reorientation. With its new Strategic Concept, the first since 2010, NATO defined and reinforced its values, purpose and goals. The core tasks of the alliance remain the same: deterrence and defence, crisis prevention and cooperative security. These tasks have been adapted to the new security policy context. Intended as a signal of transatlantic unity, the new concept adopted at the summit clearly identifies Russia as 'the greatest and most immediate threat to the security of allies and to peace and stability in the Euro-Atlantic area'. Among the concrete decisions taken at the summit was the decision to increase NATO's rapid response force to around 300,000 soldiers. The concept emphasizes transatlantic unity and makes it clear that no one should doubt NATO's strength or its determination to defend the alliance across its territories. The threat from China is also clearly stated for the first time. NATO is deliberately keeping its door open and wants to focus in particular on its partnerships with Bosnia-Herzegovina, Georgia and Ukraine. However, the key role of the United States in leading transatlantic security policy also makes the future priorities of the alliance dependent on the uncertainties associated with the next US presidential administration. At the end of the war, Ukraine may find itself in a negotiation position not unlike that of March 2022, when it demanded strong security guarantees in return for neutrality. These guarantees will not be easy to define, as they would need to include a credible military dimension in the case of any new aggression against Ukraine. The more they resemble the NATO Article-5 guarantees, the more some NATO member states will argue that it defeats the purpose to establish a parallel security architecture outside the NATO system.

International (dis)order

The consequences of the war can also be considered in terms of the learning processes taking place at the national and international levels. Not only among the elites, but also in societies, especially in Europe, a rethinking is underway in many places, especially with regard to concepts such as security and peace. This process can be described as the geopoliticization of European societies. In Western Europe in particular, the hope was that peace could be maintained through a variety of interdependencies, especially of an economic nature, as encapsulated in the EC/EU and in energy relations with Russia. Russia's invasion of Ukraine has called the foundations of this policy into question. Thinking of peace and security increasingly in terms of a military capacity represents a profound shift in fundamental principles, especially in Germany. At the end of February 2022, Chancellor Olaf Scholz proclaimed a 'time shift' (*Zeitenwende*) in the Bundestag. The term was initially associated with the unprecedented government decision on arms deliveries to Ukraine and a special fund of 100 billion euros for the modernization of the German armed forces, but it has since become a call for a more comprehensive rethinking of Germany's role in Europe, the EU's role in the world, and a broader conception of Europe in defence policy. Inside the EU, in addition to a general feeling of uncertainty, the previously abstract idea of systemic competition between democracies and autocracies is now a reality. At the same time, it can be seen that such a simple comparison of political systems is not congruent with voting behaviour on UN resolutions and (non-)participation in Western sanctions. The systemic conflict is rather between countries that were formerly colonizers, mainly in Europe and North America, and those who were colonized by Western powers. Anti-Western and anti-colonialist rhetoric is deliberately used by the Russian government in its propaganda, in an attempt to appeal to regions where the West has traditionally been viewed with mistrust. As Russia's political and economic relations with the West have been torn asunder, so its political and economic relations with the Global South have strengthened. Russia now uses those relations as leverage against the West. The historical irony inherent in Russia's contemporary neo-imperialism is of secondary importance to many governments in the Global South. The speech of the Kenyan ambassador to the UN, Martin Kimani, at the first UN General Assembly meeting after the full-scale invasion – in which he called on his African colleagues in particular not to tolerate a new imperialism in the form of Russia's war of aggression precisely because of their own experiences with colonialism – did not express a majority opinion in the region.

With regard to the energy dependencies that exist between democracies and autocracies, a diversification of strategic risk has now become indispensable. Allowing too much dependence on Russian energy sources and putting parts of the energy infrastructure into the hands of Russian state-owned enterprises has proven to be naive in terms of security policy in Germany and elsewhere in Europe. Alternative energy sources are now being developed at full speed, including ramped-up liquefied gas deliveries and an accelerated expansion of renewable energies, in particular after Russia stopped supplying gas to most EU countries at the end of August 2022.

The biggest geopolitical shift manifesting itself during Russia's war against Ukraine is the closer relationship between China and Russia. Russia may be seen as a junior partner by China, but this new 'no-limits partnership', declared during

Putin's visit to Beijing ahead of the Olympic Games in early February 2022, spells an end to the long-standing US policy of keeping Russia and China apart. As the US–China and US–Russia relationships have grown more confrontational in recent years, so Russia and China have been drawn into a closer strategic partnership going beyond pragmatic economic cooperation and including political and military dimensions. Both countries share an interest in a multipolar world order and a sense of civilizational superiority vis-à-vis 'the West'. China has not only abstained in the UN resolutions on the war, it also avoids the word 'war' altogether, speaking instead of the 'Ukraine crisis'; it straddles an ambiguous line between insisting on its own sovereignty vis-à-vis Taiwan while effectively denying sovereignty to Ukraine.

Another learning process concerns an understanding – already sharpened by the Covid-19 pandemic and now further developed – of the numerous global interconnections that are only consciously perceived in times of crisis. Western sanctions against Russia and Russia's counter-sanctions quickly led to gaps in global production and supply chains that cannot be fixed quickly. These supply chains have proven most critical in the area of food supply. The war has exacerbated the supply situation on global food markets, which had already been strained by the pandemic. Russia is the world's largest exporter of wheat and fertilizer, while Ukraine is the main exporter of sunflower oil and the fourth largest supplier of maize. Trade in these commodities has been severely disrupted by the war. In the period from 2015 to 2020, the combined export shares for sunflower oil of Russia and Ukraine stood at 66 per cent, for wheat 28 per cent, for maize 15 per cent and for fertilizers 16 per cent. Prices increased significantly on international agricultural markets for food, feed and fertilizer due to Russia's blockade of Ukraine, the sanctions on Russia, and supply stoppages and shortages in the Black Sea region.

The countries most directly affected are those in the MENA region (North Africa and the Middle East) and sub-Saharan Africa, where wheat is one of the most important staple foods and dependence on Russian and Ukrainian wheat supplies is particularly high. An immediate consequence of the war was that about 200 million people already affected by malnutrition were facing a worsening food crisis, for example in Egypt, Libya, Mauritania, Sudan, Tunisia, Lebanon and Yemen. In the medium term, countries that are less import-dependent could also be affected if domestic prices for wheat adjust to world market prices. All over the world, societies and politicians are being reminded that food security cannot be taken for granted. The consequences of failures in national and international agricultural policy have come to the fore as a result of the war. Central and East European countries such as Poland and Slovakia have reacted with import bans on Ukrainian wheat in order to protect their own agricultural sectors and reduce the risk of political opposition in an election year. Even in advanced Western countries the war has caused supply chain shortages and a surge in production costs, leading to spiralling inflation and, more recently, strikes in some European countries.

The war has had a direct impact on Ukraine's and Russia's neighbouring states. Belarus played an important role in Russia's preparations for war, after several months of mass mobilization following the rigged presidential elections in August 2020 – which Belarusian President Aleksandr Lukashenko was able to defeat, backed by the security apparatus and with Russian help. Lukashenko's dependence on Russia gave Putin the opportunity to expand the Russian military presence in Belarus. The attack on Kyiv in the first days of the invasion was led from Belarus. Even if the Belarusian military is not used, or is used only to a limited extent, it is clear whose side Belarus is on politically under Lukashenko. A large part of Belarusian society distanced itself from the state in the course of the mass protests and their suppression. Trust in the country's state institutions had already been permanently weakened. The war continues this trend and has made the division between state and society even greater. There have been small gestures of support for Ukraine, as far as this is possible in a system based on brutal repression. One risk highlighted by Belarusian activists in exile is that the EU and Western partners generally will pay less attention to Belarus, and that the impression of active support by Belarusians for Putin could even grow in Western societies. Putin is pushing for greater military integration with Belarus. In early 2023, he announced that the Russian Iskander missile system, which is capable of carrying nuclear warheads, had been moved to Belarus. A storage facility for a tactical nuclear weapon is apparently due to open in July 2023, thereby heightening insecurities on the Belarus-NATO border.

The war has also had a direct impact on Russian-backed de facto states such as Transnistria in Moldova and Abkhazia and South Ossetia in Georgia. A Russian military garrison has been stationed in Transnistria since the end of the Soviet Union. The more concrete prospect of EU membership for Moldova will also revive the status issue in Transnistria and fuel fears of direct Russian influence or escalation. Azerbaijan reignited its confrontation with Armenia over Nagorno Karabakh by blocking the corridor that links Armenia and Nagorno-Karabakh from December 2022, testing its new room for manoeuvre while Russia is not in a position to actively support Armenia. Turkey and Iran are also intent on extending their respective regional influence. Countries with a large Russian or Russian-speaking minority, such as Kazakhstan (an authoritarian system in its own right), fear growing Russian influence in the wake of the war that could endanger their internal stability. Ultimately, the extension of Russia's neo-imperial policy to other neighbouring states depends on whether Putin achieves a successful outcome in Ukraine. For the time being, Russia's neighbours, and members of Russia-led organizations like the Eurasian Economic Union, are pursuing a cautious wait-and-see policy.

Outlook

March 28, 1:48 pm
[. . .]
People are a little tired, yet they aren't intimidated.
They live, love, and won't give up. And it goes without saying –
Ukrainian flags flutter over the city. :)

            Serhiy Zhadan, *Sky Above Kharkiv* (2022)

For over a year Ukraine has been everywhere – in the ubiquitous images and reports of war, in the blue and yellow flags of solidarity integrated into our cityscapes, in everyday encounters with displaced Ukrainians, in discussions about weapons systems and arms deliveries and in concerns about the wider socioeconomic costs of the war beyond Ukraine. It is hard to think of a more tragic way for a country to inscribe itself into the mental landscape of Europe and the world. This process is linked to the recognition of (post-)imperial patterns underpinning Western European and US thinking that for too long equated the Soviet Union with Russia and removed the countries of Eastern and Central Europe, with all their political and cultural diversity, from view.

    This recognition highlights the need for a critical reappraisal of the incoherent policy adopted by several EU member states towards Russia. In Germany, the security dimension of the massive Nord Stream 2 project was downplayed for many years, and was still regarded as an acceptable economic risk until shortly before Russia's large-scale war of aggression. Despite financial support for the reform processes in Ukraine, the perspectives and security perceptions of many East and Central European states, and even US concerns about Europe's energy dependence on Russia, were subordinated to the imperative of maintaining 'good' or at least manageable relations with Russia. The challenge now is to decolonize the Western view of the Eastern European region as a whole.

Russia's war against Ukraine clearly shows that a post-imperial era did not automatically begin in Eastern Europe in 1991. The disintegration of the Soviet Union is too often described as having been largely 'peaceful'. This relativizing assumption was already incorrect in the 1990s, given the wars in Nagorny Karabakh, Transnistria, Abkhazia, South Ossetia and Chechnya. With the exception of Transnistria, all these regions went through repeated cycles of violent conflict. It has a lot to do with Western perception that these unresolved conflicts were viewed as small, geopolitically unimportant or at least reliably frozen. It can now be seen with clarity how short-sighted such assumptions were. The moment of the collapse of the Soviet Union is becoming less and less significant in retrospect; at the same time, an awareness of the medium- and long-term processes that followed that collapse – up to and including Russia's war against Ukraine – is growing.

The war against Ukraine did not begin on 24 February 2022, but eight years earlier. The annexation of Crimea, the war in the Donbas and the full-scale invasion are three phases in one war. The emergence of Ukraine as a nation and a united state did not begin only with the current war. The process began at the latest with independence in 1991 and has been marked by repeated cycles of protests and transformation.

This small book began with an attempt at an explanation. Instead of a deterministic interpretation focusing on Putin as a person, it has listed the interlocking developments that, in their interaction, made the war in its various forms possible. Vladimir Putin was the catalyst who repeatedly gave the order for war against the background of these developments. Russia's authoritarianism, which became more centralized, personalized and neo-imperial under Putin, confronted the political and civic counter-model of a democratic state in Ukraine. This harboured domestic and foreign policy risks. For Putin, both had to be averted in time and a return to the old greatness had to go down in Russian history as his legacy. The paradox of his decision to go to war is that the risks for his authoritarian system have become greater instead of smaller because of the inherent uncertainties of war and the prospect of ultimate failure.

The first part of this book was based on concepts that are central to Ukraine: independence, regional diversity, protest and democratic transformation. It highlighted common misconceptions about the ethnic, linguistic and regional identities in Ukraine, and tracked the long-standing development and mechanisms of the authoritarian system in Putin's Russia. The second part discussed the Crimean annexation, the war in Donbas and the war of aggression since February 2022 as three phases of Russia's war against Ukraine, and outlined the evolving consequences of these phases.

An end to the war is not currently in sight. Most importantly, for Ukraine there is at present no basis for negotiations, and for Russia there is (as yet) no need for them. From a historical perspective, it is not uncommon for wars to smoulder over a long period of time, gaining or losing intensity in phases. The war in Iraq lasted seven years, and the war in Afghanistan for some twenty. The 'Russo-Turkish-Wars' are an historical example of a war fought in several protracted stages.

It is clearly too early for a definitive conclusion to a book such as this. But we can end with a reflection on the mood in

Ukraine. Amidst all the destruction, war crimes and displacement, positive emotions dominate in opinion polls. According to a March 2022 Rating Group survey, for example, 90 per cent of respondents stated that they felt hopeful when thinking about the situation in Ukraine. Before the war, only one third felt hopeful. A survey by the Kyiv International Institute of Sociology in October–November 2022 found that just under 80 per cent of Ukrainians voiced optimism about the future of their country. Whether or not this is a sentiment born out of a sense of civic duty, or a psychological coping mechanism, or a true reflection of a deeply rooted optimism, we may never know. But one thing is clear – it is remarkable.

Sources and Literature

Primary Sources

Aljazeera (2022) 'Russia-Ukraine crisis: Zelensky's address in full'. Available at: https://www.aljazeera.com/news/2022/2/24/russia-ukraine-crisis-president-zelenskky-speech-in-full

Bloomberg News (2022) 'Full translation of Vladimir Putin's Victory Day speech'. Available at: https://www.bloomberg.com/news/articles/2022-05-09/full-transcript-here-s-russian-president-vladimir-putin-s-victory-day-speech#xj4y7vzkg?leadSource=uverify%20wall

CNN (2022) 'Zelensky receives standing ovation after speech to European Parliament'. Available at: https://www.youtube.com/watch?v=hVvkdwksxMw

Official Internet Resources of the President of Russia (2022a) 'Address by the President of the Russian Federation – 21.2.2022'. Available at: http://en.kremlin.ru/events/president/news/67828

Official Internet Resources of the President of Russia (2022b) 'Address by the President of the Russian Federation – 24.2.2022'. Available at: http://en.kremlin.ru/events/president/news/67843

Official Website of the President of Ukraine (2022a) 'Russia has launched a new military operation against our state, martial law is being imposed throughout Ukraine'. Available at: https://www.

president.gov.ua/en/news/rosiya-rozpochala-novu-vijskovu-oper
aciyu-proti-nashoyi-derz-73105

Official Website of the President of Ukraine (2022b) 'Address by the President of Ukraine'. Available at: https://www.president.gov.ua/ en/news/zvernennya-prezidenta-ukrayini-73137

Official Website of the President of Ukraine (2022c) 'Address by President of Ukraine Volodymyr Zelenskyy to the Bundestag'. Available at: https://www.president.gov.ua/en/news/promova-prezidenta-ukrayini-volodimira-zelenskogo-u-bundesta-73621

Putin, V. (2021) 'Offen sein trotz der Vergangenheit, Ein Gastbeitrag'. *Die Zeit/Zeit Online*. Available at: https://www.zeit.de/politik/aus land/2021-06/ueberfall-auf-die-sowjetunion-1941-europa-russla nd-geschichte-wladimir-putin/komplettansicht

UNHCR (2023) 'Operational Data Portal: Ukraine refugee situation'. Available at: https://data.unhcr.org/en/situations/ukraine

United Nations (2023) 'The UN and the war in Ukraine: Key informa-tion'. Available at: https://unric.org/en/the-un-and-the-war-in-uk raine-key-information/#uk2

Surveys

InfoSapiens (no date) 'Publications'. Available at: https://www.sapi ens.com.ua/en/publications

Kyiv International Institute of Sociology – KIIS (2014a) 'Nationwide public opinion survey: Attitudes to the unitary state and autonomy in Ukraine, April-May 2014'. Available at: https://www.kiis.com .ua/?lang=eng&cat=reports&id=319&page=6

Kyiv International Institute of Sociology – KIIS (2014b) 'The views and opinions of the residents of south-eastern regions of Ukraine, April 2014'. Available at: https://www.kiis.com.ua/?lang=eng&cat =reports&id=302&page=1&y=2014&m=4

New Europe Center (2023) 'Wartime diplomacy. What Ukrainians think about Ukraine's movement towards EU membership and beyond'. Kyiv. Available at: http://neweurope.org.ua/en/analytics/ yevropejska-integratsiya-voyennogo-chasu-shho-dumayut-ukra yintsi-pro-ruh-ukrayiny-do-yes

Onuch, O. et al. (2019–2022) MOBILISE 2019–2022: Ukrainian Nationally Representative Survey (Waves 1–3).

ZOiS (2019) 'Donbas Surveys'; for results see: Sasse, G. and Lackner, A. (2019) 'Attitudes and Identities across the Donbas Front Line: What Has Changed from 2016 to 2019?' ZOiS, Report 3. Available at: https://www.zois-berlin.de/fileadmin/media/Dateien/3-Publi kationen/ZOiS_Reports/2019/ZOiS_Report_3_2019.pdf

Other Literature

Arel, D. and Driscoll, J. (2022) *Ukraine's Unnamed War: Before the Russian Invasion of 2022*. Cambridge: Cambridge University Press.

Balmaceda, M. M. (2021) *Russian Energy Chains: The Remaking of Technopolitics from Siberia to Ukraine to the European Union*. New York: Columbia University Press.

Beichelt, T. and Worschech, S. (2017) *Transnational Ukraine? Networks and Ties that Influence(d) Contemporary Ukraine*. Stuttgart: ibidem.

Beissinger, M. R. (2022) *The Revolutionary City: Urbanization and the Global Transformation of Rebellion*. Princeton, NJ: Princeton University Press.

Bidenko, Y. (2018) '(De)structuring of the Civil Society in the Political Process in Ukraine and Belarus'. In Smith, D. H., Moldavanova, A. V. and Krasynska, S. (eds.), *The Nonprofit Sector in Eastern Europe, Russia and Central Asia: Civil Society Advances and Challenges*. Leiden: Brill, 29–55.

Channell-Justice, E. (2022) *Without the State: Self-Organization and Political Activism in Ukraine*. Toronto: University of Toronto Press.

Charap, S. and Colton, T. J. (2018) *Everyone Loses: The Ukraine Crisis and the Ruinous Contest for Post-Soviet Eurasia*. Abingdon: Routledge.

D'Anieri, P. (2019) *Ukraine and Russia: From Civilized Divorce to Uncivil War*. Cambridge: Cambridge University Press.

dekoder, Centre for East European and International Studies – ZOiS and The Research Centre for East European Studies – FSO (2019)

'The Crimean Archipelago: Overview'. Available at: https://crimea.dekoder.org/archipelago

Dollbaum, J. M., Lallouet M., and Noble, B. (2021) *Navalny: Putin's Nemesis, Russia's Future?* London: C. Hurst & Co.

Dragneva, R. and Wolczuk, K. (2015) *Ukraine between the EU and Russia: The Integration Challenge.* New York: Palgrave Macmillan.

Fischer, S. (2022) 'Peace Talks between Russia and Ukraine: Mission Impossible'. Berlin: Stiftung Wissenschaft und Politik, SWP-Comment No. 65 (November). Available at: https://www.swp-berlin.org/publications/products/comments/2022C65_PeaceTalksRussia_Ukraine.pdf

Frye, T. (2021) *Weak Strongman.* Princeton, NJ: Princeton University Press.

Giuliano, E. (2018) 'Who Supported Separatism in Donbas? Ethnicity and Popular Opinion at the Start of the Ukraine Crisis'. In Onuch, O., Hale H. E. and Sasse, G. (eds.), Special Issue: 'Identity Politics in Times of Crisis: Ukraine as a Critical Case'. *Post-Soviet Affairs* 34:2–3, pp. 158–78.

Glauben, T. et al (2022) 'The War in Ukraine Exposes Supply Tensions on Global Agricultural Markets: Openness to Global Trade is Needed to Cope with the Crisis'. IAMO Policy Brief No. 44, Halle (Saale).

Greene, S. A. and Robertson, G. B. (2019) *Putin v. the People: The Perilous Politics of a Divided Russia.* New Haven, CT: Yale University Press.

Harding, L. (2022) *Invasion: The Inside Story of Russia's Bloody War and Ukraine's Fight for Survival.* New York: Vintage Books.

Hurak, I. and D'Anieri, P. (2022) 'The Evolution of Russian Political Tactics in Ukraine'. *Problems of Post-Communism* 69:2, pp. 121–32.

IISS (2023) 'Country focus: Ukraine'. Available at: https://www.iiss.org/regions/russia-and-eurasia/ukraine

ISW (2022) 'Ukraine conflict updates'. Available at: https://understandingwar.org/backgrounder/ukraine-conflict-updates

Keudel, O. (2022) *How Patronal Networks Shape Opportunities for Local Citizen Participation in a Hybrid Regime. A Comparative Analysis of Five Cities in Ukraine.* Stuttgart: ibidem/Columbia University Press.

Khromeychuk, O. (2021) *A Loss: The Story of a Dead Soldier Told by His Sister.* Stuttgart: ibidem.

Kostiuchenko, T. and Martsenyuk, T. (2022) *Russia's War in Ukraine 2022: Personal Experiences of Ukrainian Scholars.* Stuttgart: ibidem.

Kulyk, V. (2018) 'Shedding Russianness, Recasting Ukrainianness: The Post-Euromaidan Dynamics of Ethnonational Identifications in Ukraine'. In Onuch, O., Hale, H. E. and Sasse, G. (eds.), Special Issue: 'Identity Politics in Times of Crisis: Ukraine as a Critical Case'. *Post-Soviet Affairs* 34:2–3, pp. 119–38.

Kulyk, V. (2019) 'Identity in Transformation: Russian-Speakers in Post-Soviet Ukraine'. *Europe-Asia Studies* 71:1, pp. 156–78.

Kurkov, A. (2014) *Ukraine Diaries: Dispatches From Kiev.* London: Harvill Secker.

Kuznetsova, I. and Mikheieva, O. (2020) 'Forced Displacement from Ukraine's War-Torn Territories: Intersectionality and Power Geometry'. *Nationalities Papers* 48:4, pp. 690–706.

Kyiv School of Economics Institute (no date) 'KSE Institute'. Available at: https://kse.ua/kse-department/kse-institute

Löwis, S. and Sasse, G. (2021) 'A Border Regime in the Making? The Case of the Contact Line in Ukraine'. *Historical Social Research* 46:3, pp. 208–44.

McGlynn, J. (2023) *Russia's War.* Cambridge: Polity Press.

Mankoff, J. (2022) *Imperial Legacies in Eurasia: How Imperial Legacies Shape International Security.* New Haven, CT: Yale University Press.

Minakov, M., Kasianov, G. and Rojansky, M. (2021) *From 'The Ukraine' to Ukraine: A Contemporary History, 1991–2021.* Stuttgart: ibidem.

Myshlovska, O. and Schmid, U. (eds.) (2019) *Regionalism without Regions: Reconceptualizing Ukraine's Heterogeneity.* Budapest: Central European University Press.

Onuch, O. (2014) *Mapping Mass Mobilization: Understanding Revolutionary Moments in Argentina and Ukraine*. London: Palgrave Macmillan.

Onuch, O. and Hale, H. E. (2022) *The Zelensky Effect.* London: Hurst.

Onuch, O. and Sasse, G. (2016) 'The Maidan in Movement and the Cycles of Protest'. *Europe-Asia Studies* 68:4, pp. 556–87.

Onuch, O., Hale, H. E. and Sasse, G. (2018) 'Studying Identity in Ukraine'. Introduction to Special Issue: 'Identity Politics in Times of Crisis: Ukraine as a Critical Case', *Post-Soviet Affairs* 34:2–3, pp. 79–83.

Plokhy, S. (2017) *The Gates of Europe: A History of Ukraine*. New York: Basic Books.

Plokhy, S. (2022) *The Frontline: Essays on Ukraine's Past and Present*. Cambridge, MA: Harvard Ukrainian Research Institute.

Plokhy, S. (2023) *The Russo-Ukrainian War: The Return of History*. New York: Norton & Co.

Portnov, A. (2020) 'Poland and Ukraine: Entangled Histories, Asymmetric Memories'. In *Essays of the Forum Transregionale Studien*. Berlin: Forum Transregionale Studien.

Romanova, V. and Umland, A. (2019) 'Ukraine Decentralization Reforms since 2014: Initial Achievements and Future Challenges', *Chatham House Research Papers*, September. Available at: https://www.chathamhouse.org/2019/09/ukraines-decentralization-reforms-2014

Sasse, G. (2007) *The Crimea Question: Identity, Transition and Conflict*. Cambridge, MA: Harvard University Press.

Sasse, G. (2020) 'War and Displacement: The Case of Ukraine'. *Europe-Asia Studies* 72:3, pp. 347–53.

Sasse, G. (ed.) (2022/23) 'Russia's War against Ukraine: A Trio of Virtual Special Issues'. *Europe-Asia Studies* 1–3.

Sasse, G. and Lackner, A. (2019) 'War and State-Making in Ukraine: Forging a Civic Identity from Below?' *The Ideology and Politics Journal* 1:12.

Sereda, V. (2020a) 'In Search of Belonging: Rethinking the Other in the Historical Memory of Ukrainian IDPs'. *The Ideology and Politics Journal* 2:16, pp. 83–107.

Sereda, V. (2020b) '"Social Distancing" and Hierarchies of Belonging: The Case of Displaced Population from Donbas and Crimea'. In Sasse, G. (ed.) 'War and Displacement: The Case of Ukraine'. *Europe-Asia Studies* 72:3, pp. 404–31.

Sereda, V. (2023) *Displacement in War-Torn Ukraine: State, Displacement and Belonging*. Cambridge: Cambridge University Press (Online Series: Elements in Global Development Studies).

Snyder, T. (2019) *The Road to Unfreedom: Russia, Europe, America*. New York: Vintage Books.

Snyder, T. (2022) *Bloodlands: Europe Between Hitler and Stalin*. New York: Basic Books.

Szporluk, R. (2000) *Russia, Ukraine, and the Breakup of the Soviet Union*. Stanford: Hoover Institution Press.

Trebesch, C. et al. (2023) 'The Ukraine Support Tracker: Which Countries Help Ukraine and How?' Kiel Working Paper No. 2218, Kiel Institute for the World Economy. Available at: https://www .ifw-kiel.de/publications/kiel-working-papers/2022/the-ukraine -support-tracker-which-countries-help-ukraine-and-how-172 04/

Uehling, G. L. (2023) *Everyday War: The Conflict over Donbas, Ukraine*. Ithaca: Cornell University Press.

Wilson, A. (2014) *Ukraine Crisis: What It Means for the West*. New Haven, CT: Yale University Press.

Wilson, A. (2022) *The Ukrainians: Unexpected Nation*. Fifth edition. New Haven, CT: Yale University Press.

Zarembo, K. (2020) *European Donbas: How to Talk about European Integration in Donetsk and Luhansk Regions*. Kyiv: Friedrich-Ebert-Stiftung.

Zhadan, S. (2023 [2022]) *Sky Above Kharkiv: Dispatches from the Ukrainian Front*. New Haven, CT: Yale University Press.

Zhurzhenko, T. (2010) *Borderlands into Bordered Lands: Geopolitics of Identity in Post-Soviet Ukraine*. Stuttgart: ibidem.

Zhurzhenko, T., Fedor, J. M., Kangaspuro, M. and Lassila, J. (2017) *War and Memory in Russia, Ukraine and Belarus.* London: Palgrave Macmillan.

Index